CW00326423

THE
GLASSHOUSE
garden

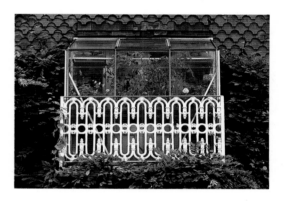

THE
GLASSHOUSE
garden

JOHN
WATKINS

conran

OCTOPUS

First published in 1993 by Conran Octopus Limited
37 Shelton Street, London WC2H 9HN

Text copyright © John Watkins 1993

Design and layout copyright © Conran Octopus Limited 1993

The right of John Watkins to be identified as author of this work
has been asserted by him in accordance with the Copyright,
Designs and Patents Act 1988.

All rights reserved. No part of this book may be reproduced,
stored in a retrieval system, or transmitted in any form or by any
means, electronic, electrostatic, magnetic tape, mechanical,
photocopying, recording, or otherwise, without the prior
permission in writing of the publisher.

A catalogue record for this book is available from the
British Library.

ISBN 1-85029-984-6

Project Editor	Jane O'Shea
Project Art Editor	Ann Burnham
Editor	Helen Ridge
Art Editor	Alistair Plumb
Picture Researcher	Jessica Walton
Editorial Assistant	Caroline Davison
Production	Sonya Sibbons
Illustrators	Shirley Felts
	Michael Shoebridge
	Christine Wilson
	Nicola Gregory
	Valerie Alford

Typeset by Servis Filmsetting Ltd, England
Printed and bound in Hong Kong

Both metric and imperial measurements are given throughout
the book except for working calculations where only metric
measurements are given. For practical usage, the conversion of
measurements from metric to imperial has, in some instances,
been rounded up or down.

FRONT JACKET *'Alicante' tomatoes.*

BACK JACKET *A glasshouse used to raise annual
bedding plants and house plants.*

PAGE 1 *Glasshouse gardening on a raised balcony
using a small lean-to structure.*

PAGE 2 *Flowering and foliage plants grown under
glass will provide year-round interest.*

RIGHT *A glasshouse can be both an attractive and a
practical asset.*

CONTENTS

GARDENING UNDER GLASS

Glasshouse cultivation is one of the most absorbing and rewarding forms of gardening for anyone who enjoys growing plants. The enthusiastic gardener can adapt the glasshouse climate to suit a particular group of plants, or raise flowers, fruit and vegetables out of their natural season. The glasshouse can also be used as an essential garden tool, enabling the keen amateur to expand the scope of plants grown in the garden, as well as save money by raising his own plants.

Glasshouse displays in botanical and public gardens can be a great source of inspiration to the small glasshouse owner for the design and choice of plants. In this winter display, tree ferns add height and style, while colour on the ground is provided by dieffenbachias and Primula obconica.

In the late nineteenth century when glasshouses were beyond the means of most people, winter gardens were built in public parks, housing exotic plants such as palms, cacti and succulents which could be enjoyed all year round.

Although the gardener is master over the glasshouse climate, he soon discovers that he is a servant to his plants, pandering to their every need, whether it be watering, feeding or potting on. It is my intention here not only to extol the pleasures of glasshouse gardening, but also to show what can be achieved in a protected environment – whether a greenhouse, conservatory or garden frame – and to describe the work involved in achieving the desired results.

Like all gardeners, glasshouse enthusiasts soon develop an interest in visiting gardens, seeing some of the great glasshouse collections and buildings and learning about the history of glasshouse cultivation. It has a very long history: there is even some evidence

to show that the Romans used frame-like structures to protect plants from the cold. However, it was not until the seventeenth and eighteenth centuries that large structures were extensively built to protect the 'greens' that were so fashionable in the wealthy households of the time. The cultivation of oranges and lemons was so popular that special 'orangeries' were designed for winter protection. These heavy structures were built of stone and wood with large windows; early orangeries, such as the one at the Oxford Botanic Garden built in 1620, were heated by portable braziers trundled around on wheels.

As building technology developed and the needs of plants were better understood, improved struc-

Conservatories became very fashionable in the late nineteenth century. They were mass produced from wood or cast iron and could be bought through mail order catalogues.

prices and were used mainly for raising plants. In recent years the popularity of conservatories attached to the house has soared; modern, double-glazing panels can provide as much insulation as a brick wall to create a comfortable living space, as well as provide an ideal environment in which to grow and display tender plants.

Although greenhouse and conservatory originally both meant a place to house or conserve greens (variegated hollies, citrus, myrtles and oleanders), today greenhouse implies a place in which plants are raised while conservatory usually describes a glazed room where plants may or may not play a significant role. Because much of what I shall be discussing applies to both greenhouses and conservatories, I have chosen to use the term glasshouse to describe any glazed structure in which plants are grown. Garden frames and cloches are included as they can be used on their own to over-winter or advance plants, or as a valuable extension to the greenhouse or conservatory providing an additional protected environment.

To help with the initial choice of a glasshouse, I will describe the siting and selection of a structure and explain the importance of different glasshouse features in obtaining the ideal growing conditions for your plants and the best value for money. Once you have set up your glasshouse, the real art lies in its management and raising the plants you want in the available space. I explain the basic principles of raising plants from seed, cuttings, division and layering. In writing about pest and disease control, I have taken into account recent environmental legislation and the resistance of pests to chemical control. From my experience over recent years, I have found that a combined offensive of mild chemicals and biological controls produces the best results.

A glasshouse can be used for so many different purposes that it is difficult to decide how to group the information about the plants that can be grown. I have chosen to divide it between two chapters: The productive glasshouse and The display glasshouse. The former describes how to use the glasshouse all

tures, with a large surface area of glass supported by iron or wooden glazing bars, were designed. By the mid-nineteenth century it had become popular to build conservatories adjacent to large houses to show off exotic plant collections; and walled gardens were edged with greenhouses to raise bedding plants, which became a central feature of Victorian gardens, and out-of-season fruit and vegetables, valuable at a time when there were no freezers.

There was a decline in large private glasshouses during the two world wars due to a shortage of materials for their maintenance and fuel to heat them. However, in the 1950s mass-produced, small greenhouses became widely available at affordable

LEFT *The tree fern*
Dicksonia antarctica *and*
the kangaroo paw
Anigozanthos manglesii
thrive in the cool, moist
atmosphere of this
splendid Victorian
glasshouse.

year round to produce out-of-season fruit and veg-etables as well as raise bedding, half-hardy and herbaceous plants, and trees and shrubs. The latter covers flowering plants of all kinds and I explain how to achieve a stunning display through the seasons. Many of the plants described – which include climbers, bulbs, chrysanthemums, begonias, pelar-goniums and flowering annuals and biennials – can be displayed to great effect in the glasshouse in which they are grown, as well as in a glazed porch or conservatory. To help balance the display and pro-ductive use of your glasshouse, a chapter divided into seasons gives a yearly view of work under glass and looks at how the plants respond to the changing seasons. In the final chapter I describe the plants that I feel make the most valuable contribution in the frost-free, temperate and tropical glasshouse.

I hope that this book will show the new gardener the incredible scope that glasshouse gardening has to offer while the experienced grower will be encour-aged to widen his horizons, and make better use of the glasshouse space.

This attractive modern
orangery, with brick pillars
supporting the roof, will
be used to over-winter the
oleanders seen here
standing outside in their
large pots.

CHOOSING YOUR GLASSHOUSE

Choosing a glasshouse and setting it up are important and expensive steps to take. This chapter aims to help you select the right glasshouse and the right site, and describes the various styles that are available. The different aspects of a glasshouse that make it a suitable environment for growing plants are also discussed, including heating, watering and staging. Although many of the points mentioned here are relevant to conservatories, the main emphasis of this chapter is on glasshouses that will be used to raise plants.

The selection and siting of a glasshouse is most important if it is to provide useful service over the years. This glasshouse is positioned close to the home, making access easier during the winter months and the installation of permanent services, such as water and electricity, less expensive.

First thoughts

A Victorian-style, free-standing glasshouse can be attractive as well as useful and, if made of modern materials such as aluminium, requires little maintenance.

Before buying a glasshouse it is important to decide what purpose it is to serve. Is it intended purely for raising plants, or as an extension to your home where only a few plants will be kept? If it is to serve as the latter, it will need to be well insulated and thoroughly waterproof, while letting in the maximum amount of light. This means that it will require a substantial framework to support large panes of glass in sealed units. To provide additional comfort, the conservatory could be fitted with double-glazed safety glass and a solid tiled floor, but this in turn will increase the cost. Indeed, where cost is not a consideration, glasshouses can be designed to any shape or form, creating beautiful structures with good light penetration and insulation, thus combining the attributes of aesthetics and function. However, if the main purpose is to grow plants, a traditional glasshouse is sufficient and will cost considerably less with its lighter structure, narrower glazing bars and, in many designs, small, unsealed panes of glass.

Even with a small, heated 1.8×2.5m (6×8ft) glasshouse it is possible to raise some bedding plants, grow a summer vegetable crop, such as tomatoes or melons, and over-winter tender plants. However, I would always advise you to select the largest structure you can afford which will fit the chosen site in your garden. Remember that the smaller your glasshouse, the more organized and disciplined you have to be. Sowings and plantings must be planned so that the plants are not all competing for space at the same time.

It is helpful to know which plants you intend growing as this, too, will affect your final choice of glasshouse. For example, if tall crops, such as tomatoes and cucumbers, are grown, or if winter vegetables, such as lettuce, are raised in the glasshouse border, a glass-to-ground model is needed. Where pot plants are grown permanently on internal benches, the glasshouse can be built on a dwarf wall to the height of the bench. The smaller surface area of glass will cost less to heat.

RIGHT *This traditional wooden glasshouse with straight sides is ideally suited to growing tall crops, such as a standard peach tree and tomatoes.*

Types of glasshouse

Glasshouses are either free-standing or lean-to, that is, built against an existing wall. A free-standing glasshouse has the advantage that, if placed in the open, it will receive full sun throughout the day and is suitable for a wide range of plants. The main disadvantage when compared with a lean-to is that more heat is lost through its larger surface area.

Lean-to glasshouses have long been used in the walled gardens of large country houses. Placed on a shady wall, a lean-to is suitable for shade-tolerant plants, such as the climber *Lapageria rosea*, and plants requiring cool, constant temperatures, such as half-hardy ferns. On a sunny wall the lean-to will receive direct sunlight all year round and is perfect for succulents. Good ventilation and shading in the spring and summer to prevent overheating are essential. The high daytime temperatures will warm the back wall which acts as a heat battery, releasing its accumulated heat at night. Plants in a glasshouse with this orientation will need the most attention as they will dry out rapidly.

Glasshouses vary considerably in their shapes and internal dimensions. Here I describe the main groups of manufactured glasshouses with the major benefits of each. You will generally pay less for mass-produced structures which usually come in self-assembly kits, while the more complicated types may need to be erected by the supplier.

Traditional glasshouses have straight sides which allow the maximum use of internal space, and are ideal for climbers. Popular models often have a wide range of additional accessories, such as purpose-built staging and hooks for wires for training plants.

Glasshouses with sloping sides have the advantage of allowing the greatest penetration of winter sun-light. The low winter sun striking the glass at 90 degrees lets in the maximum amount of light. Where the sun strikes the glass at a greater or lesser angle, a proportion of the light is reflected away from the glasshouse. Sloping sides also offer less wind resistance than straight sides and are therefore less likely to be damaged during windy weather. This type of glasshouse is most suitable for short winter crops, such as early spring lettuce, and flowering annuals from seed, which do not require much headroom.

Dutch light glasshouses have large panes of glass which cast little shade on the plants inside. They are simple to erect, consisting of frames bolted together which are supported on a steel framework for all but the smallest models. They are easy to move and extra sections can be added on to them, a useful attraction as no glasshouse is ever big enough.

Curvilinear glasshouses are designed primarily to let in the maximum amount of light throughout the year by presenting at least one side perpendicular to the sun. This attractive style of glasshouse tends to be expensive because of the number of different angles which require more engineering. Lack of height at the sides could be a drawback, although a compromise could be reached by selecting a model with straight sides and a curvilinear roof.

Uneven span glasshouses, designed for maximum light transmission on one side, are generally taller than traditional glasshouses, making them suitable for tall, early season crops, such as cucumbers.

Polygonal glasshouses are designed more as garden features than as practical growing houses, and, consequently, are expensive. Their internal space is somewhat limited and on smaller models overheating can be a problem because of their small roof ventilators. They are more suitable for growing

Glasshouse shapes

Straight-sided

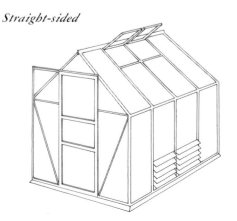

Dutch light

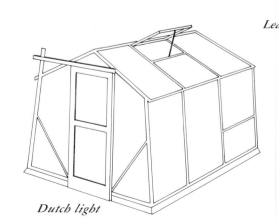

Lean-to

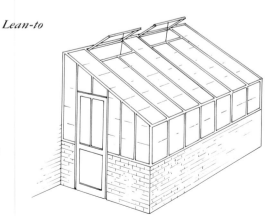

A lean-to glasshouse built on to the sunny side of the house warms up quickly in the sun and can conveniently be linked to the household heating system and water supply.

RIGHT *A traditional Dutch light glasshouse with sloping sides, large panes of glass and few glazing bars is ideal for light-demanding winter crops.*

smaller pot plants, such as pelargoniums and cacti.

Solar glasshouses are designed primarily for areas with very cold winters and poor winter light. They take the form of lean-to structures facing the sun, are well insulated to conserve heat and are sometimes partially sunk into the ground. They are particularly suitable for winter vegetable crops and early-sown bedding plants, such as begonias and pelargoniums.

Mini lean-to glasshouses are suitable for small gardens where space is limited, or they can be used to create a separate environment within larger glasshouses. The space inside is large enough to grow two tomato or melon plants in growing bags, or you can install shelves to provide a multi-layered growing environment, ideal for many small potted plants and raising summer bedding plants.

Curvilinear

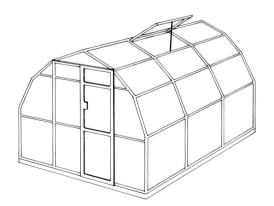

Polygonal

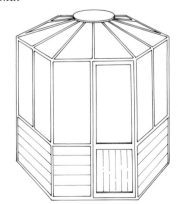

Uneven span

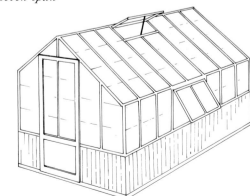

ABOVE *Traditional barn cloches are useful for warming up the ground for early crops of lettuce or providing a protected environment for exotic crops such as sweet peppers, as illustrated here.*

RIGHT *A cold frame with a brick base is perfect for hardening off garden plants. By sliding open the frame light, plants are gradually acclimatized to outside conditions.*

Cloches

Cloches are the simplest glazed structures for protecting plants. They may be used singly to cover one garden plant or butted together to protect, for example, a whole row of early seedlings or strawberries. The two main types of glass cloche are the tent cloche, assembled from two panes of glass, and the taller, barn cloche assembled from four panes of glass. The panes of both types are secured with metal clips or wires. In recent years, glass cloches have been superseded by plastic models. Semi-rigid corrugated plastic sheeting bent over rows of plants and secured with wire hoops, and the cheaper and more popular low polythene tunnel supported over a row of wire hoops, are two of the most common types. Tunnels are available in widths from 75cm (2½ft) to 2m (6½ft). The ends are secured by burying them in the ground, and ventilation is provided by raising the polythene sides.

Cold frames

Cold frames are usually no more than 60–120cm (2–4ft) high with either solid, well-insulated sides made of brick or wood, or transparent sides made of plastic or glass supported by an aluminium or wooden framework. A frame light or lid, made up of a wooden or metal frame glazed in a variety of materials, is held in place on top of the base. Frames are often designed so that their lights are angled, allowing the rain to run off and increasing the amount of natural light let in. When positioning the frame, make sure that the lower front side of the frame faces the sun so that less shade is cast on the plants inside. Important points to consider are the weight of the frame as those made of light materials, such as plastic, are easily blown about and damaged. For frost protection wood- and brick-based frames have the best insulation properties. An unheated frame is most useful for hardening off tender plants as the lights can be opened wider and wider to allow more air to enter, and can take the pressure off limited space in the glasshouse. Frames may be used for the propagation of both seed and cuttings and, with the addition of heating in the form of soil-heating cables can be used to raise and over-winter tender plants.

Siting your glasshouse

Ideally, a glasshouse should be sited in a sheltered position away from any buildings or trees that may cast shade. Falling leaves and branches and root invasion are also important reasons for not choosing a site close to trees. If the glasshouse is to be used in winter, it will need to be positioned so that the plants will be provided with as much sunlight as possible, which is vital for healthy plant growth. Remember that the sun is lower in the sky during winter and casts longer shadows.

It is best to site the glasshouse on a compass bearing so that one long side will face the direction of the sun. If this is not done, the roof will cast more shade on the plants inside.

Protection should be provided from prevailing winds as cold winds blowing over a glasshouse in winter will greatly increase the heat loss and place added strain on the heating system. Avoid siting the glasshouse in frost hollows where cold air collects and cannot drain away. Such areas can be quite a few degrees colder than where there is good air drainage.

Although fixed supplies of water, electricity and gas are not essential to the glasshouse gardener, they can make life simpler. However, as they are expensive to install, you may prefer to place the glasshouse as close as possible to the house and use existing supplies (see page 23). This will also make access to the glasshouse easier during bad weather.

Before making any firm decisions on where to position your glasshouse, you should check whether any planning permission is required or if certain building regulations apply.

CHECKLIST

- Most growers soon discover that their glasshouses are too small for their needs.
- The glasshouse door should be wide enough and high enough to allow easy access.
- The door should not have too large a lip at the base which would make wheelbarrow access difficult.
- A generous ground-to-eaves height maximizes growing space and provides enough height to work in without stooping.
- Glasshouses with sloping sides let in more light than straight-sided houses, but at the expense of internal space.
- Internal supports will be necessary if you intend placing your glasshouse on an exposed site.
- Similar glasshouses produced by different manufacturers can differ widely in price.

WINDBREAKS

Place windbreaks perpendicular to the direction of the wind, ensuring they cast no shade on the glasshouse. Avoid solid windbreaks, such as brick walls, as the wind will be forced up over the wall causing turbulence immediately to leeward, which can result in damage to the glasshouse. Trees and hedges are the most attractive windbreaks, although purpose-built barriers, usually of plastic strips or fabric, are the most effective. Ideally, the minimum length of a windbreak should be 12 times its height and the minimum distance from the glasshouse four times windbreak height.

Easy access to this traditional-style, wooden and half-brick glasshouse is provided by a gravel path – a particularly valuable asset in winter when grass and soil paths are often permanently wet under foot.

Construction materials

Wood and aluminium are the two most popular materials used for small glasshouses. Steel is used for larger structures and UPVC for conservatories.

Wood

CHECKLIST

When selecting any type of glasshouse, it is important to check that:
- All joints are well made and fit snugly.
- The glazing bars and ridge are sturdy and not sagging.
- The glass fits the frames properly and neither leaves gaps where water can enter nor has wide overlaps of glass, making cleaning difficult.

This is the most attractive material used for glasshouses. It should be close grained, free of knots and splits and resistant to decay. Softwood is used for all but the most expensive glasshouses which are made of seasoned oak or teak, and have the advantage of being long-lasting and needing little maintenance. Western red cedar is probably the best softwood for smaller glasshouses, its poor bulk-to-strength ratio making it unsuitable for large glasshouses. It has a natural resistance to decay and, although more expensive, can last a lifetime if well looked after. Softwoods cheaper than western red cedar are available for both large and small glasshouses, but they will decay more easily unless they have been pressure-treated with preservatives. Your supplier should be able to advise you on this point. If properly maintained, they can last from 20–30 years. Softwoods that have not been pressure-treated should have preservative applied at least every two years to protect them from damp and decaying organisms.

Paintwork will need to be checked regularly and repainted every two or three years.

The base of a wooden glasshouse is often the first part to deteriorate. This may be caused by condensation dripping off the glass in cool weather or the build-up of moist soil around the base. To prevent this, the base should be raised above the soil on bricks and guttering installed to take the rain off the roof and keep the soil around the base dry.

Glazing bars

As wood is a poor conductor of heat, the glazing bars remain warm, thus reducing condensation. However, they tend to be wider than their aluminium counterparts and cast more shadow. Accessories are easily fitted to the bars with nails, screws or pins but make sure they are made from brass or galvanized steel, otherwise they may deteriorate before the wood. Dry glazing systems are also used in some designs of wooden glasshouses (see below).

Aluminium alloy

This useful material does not require regular maintenance and will not normally corrode; instead it oxidizes at its surface to form a fine protective layer.

Types of glazing bar

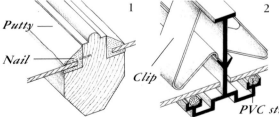

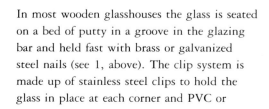

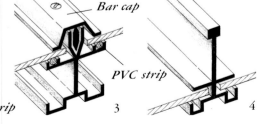

In most wooden glasshouses the glass is seated on a bed of putty in a groove in the glazing bar and held fast with brass or galvanized steel nails (see 1, above). The clip system is made up of stainless steel clips to hold the glass in place at each corner and PVC or mastic strips to cushion it (see 2, above). The bar cap system holds the glass firmly to the glazing bar with a continuous bar cap (see 3, above). In a dry glazing system the glass is slotted into a groove in the glazing bar without the use of sealants (see 4, above).

On expensive glasshouses the bare aluminium may be powder-coated to give an attractive, non-metallic finish, available in a wide range of colours. Sturdy structures can last up to 100 years, while light-weight models may buckle and last only 30 years.

Glazing bars

Aluminium glazing bars are narrower than wooden glazing bars and create less internal shade. The cheapest method of securing glass to an aluminium glazing bar is with the clip system (see opposite). The disadvantage of this system is that as the glass is held only at each corner, it can crack and be blown out in high winds if the tension is uneven. In dry areas the wind may deposit dirt and dust particles in the drip channels between the glass and the glazing bar, and moss will establish itself, creating severe drip problems.

The aluminium bar cap system (see opposite) prevents airborne debris blowing in, reducing the growth of moss. PVC caps are available that will press on to existing clip glazing bars to gain the advantages of a bar cap system.

With many of the cheaper glazing systems a significant part of the glazing bar sits outside the glasshouse. The large surface area exposed to the cold air can result in as much as a 10 per cent heat loss inside the glasshouse. A low profile glazing system has been developed so that only the PVC bar cap is exposed outside the glasshouse and, as PVC is a poor conductor of heat, much less heat is lost. Dry glazing systems are also used on some aluminium glasshouses (see opposite).

Steel

Steel has the advantage of high tensile strength and a good strength-to-bulk ratio, which means that it is an ideal building material for larger glasshouses. Only consider steel glasshouses that have been galvanized or treated with rust-preventive paint. If galvanized, make sure that it is not wearing thin and never buy a glasshouse that shows any sign of rust.

Equivalent steel and aluminium glasshouses have similar lifespans, although this will be reduced considerably for a steel structure if rust is not attended to. In steel glasshouses, the glass is held in place with either putty, bitumen or in a dry-glazing system (see opposite).

UPVC

UPVC (rigid polyvinyl chloride) which is used mainly in conservatory building will not decay or rust and is therefore maintenance-free. However, after a period of time it can become abraded by dirt in the atmosphere and lose its smart finish. With larger conservatories, where a considerable amount of weight needs supporting, the UPVC framework is often strengthened with the insertion of a metal core. As UPVC is not inherently strong, the glazing bars, which are made to a high specification and can vary in design from conservatory to conservatory, will need to be as thick as wooden glazing bars, some-times even thicker, and will be able to support only a lightweight plastic roof.

The wooden glazing bars of this conservatory have been painted white so that the light is reflected back off the bars on to the plants. White paint also increases the impression of a light and airy structure.

Cladding materials

(see page 20)

ERECTING THE GLASSHOUSE

Make sure you receive clear instructions from the manufacturer on how to erect the framework and insert the glazing. Whether you erect the glasshouse yourself or get your supplier or local builder to do it for you, the following guidelines should help.

● Choose a firm, level site that is well drained.

● Erect the glasshouse on a calm, dry day.

● Complete the cladding in one day.

● If plants are to be grown in the glasshouse soil, take care not to compact the site.

● Leave ducting for the provision of water, gas and electricity when laying foundations.

● Stack and retain good topsoil removed during excavation for use within the glasshouse or garden.

● If the ground is wet, lay drains to a sump, dug at the far end of the glasshouse.

● Where a drainage problem persists, raise the beds above ground level.

● Lay a path – simple concrete, paved or wooden slatted duckboards – inside the glasshouse.

Once you have selected the glasshouse structure, you must consider the type of cladding – whether to use traditional glass or modern plastic. While glasshouses clad in plastic offer the cheapest form of protection, glass is the most aesthetically pleasing of the two materials and the most usual choice for many greenhouse and conservatory structures.

Glass

Most glasshouses are clad with 3mm (⅛in) thick glass, which is cheap, easy to clean, and not readily scratched; it is, however, heavy and rather brittle. The panes usually measure 60×60cm (2×2ft) in traditional glasshouses (some wooden types have even smaller panes) or 1.5×0.75m ($5 \times 2\frac{1}{2}$ft) in Dutch light glasshouses. The small panes require less support and can be held in with clips at each corner (see page 20), while the Dutch light sheets are usually mounted into frames in a dry glazing system, which support the glass on all sides. The large areas of glass are, of course, more expensive to replace if broken and the unit size can restrict the design style, especially on smaller houses.

If the glasshouse is used purely for horticultural purposes, 3mm (⅛in) glass is perfectly adequate. However, if there are young children in the family, it is advisable to fit toughened glass to the sides and door. Where the glasshouse is attached to a house, and especially if it is used as a living room, a laminated glass or plastic roof should be considered as falling snow or tiles from the house roof on to ordinary glass could lead to tragic consequences.

Plastic

Plastic-based materials are often supplied as large, lightweight sheets which cast less shade inside the glasshouse because fewer and thinner glazing bars are needed. Plastic-clad glasshouses are more airtight than their glass equivalents and this in turn helps to conserve heat. Plastic is flexible and can be shaped, drilled, bolted or screwed without shattering, and

this safety aspect alone has led to its increasing popularity over the past few years.

Early plastic cladding systems degraded rapidly, sometimes within a year, due to UV (ultraviolet) light, but modern plastics contain a UV inhibitor to extend their lifespan. However, such plastic is not easily cleaned and dirt will build up on the surface, drastically reducing light transmission.

Rigid or semi-rigid sheets

Glass-reinforced polyester has a very good light transmission (86–92 per cent). It is available in flat and corrugated sheets, often coated with a sheet of polyvinyl fluoride to reduce solar deterioration.

Polycarbonate has a light transmission of up to 80 per cent and is available in double or triple thickness. It is treated against deterioration by the sun and some manufacturers guarantee no more than a six per cent loss in light transmission over a 10-year period. Some manufacturers also offer a five-year warranty against hail damage.

Acrylic has a light transmission of 85 per cent, is more brittle than polycarbonate and so can develop cracks if held too tightly in the frame. It is available in single or double thickness.

Flexible sheets

Fluoroplastic film has an excellent light transmission (95 per cent), and is resistant to ultraviolet degradation and extremes of temperature. In addition, it retains heat well.

Polythene (polyethylene) is the cheapest form of cladding. It has a very good light transmission (86–90 per cent) but, unless anti-fogging additives are present, condensation can reduce light transmission to as little as 78 per cent in summer and 60 per cent in winter. Most polythenes used in horticulture contain a UV inhibitor which allows the polythene to be used for two, three or four seasons without it becoming yellow and brittle. On clear nights, up to 80 per cent of heat can be lost, sometimes resulting in the inside of the structure being colder than the outside.

Services

Water

Water 'on tap' within the glasshouse is a valuable asset. As well as making the filling of a watering can more convenient, it allows the use of automatic and semi-automatic watering systems and is necessary for mist propagation which requires a pressurized water supply. Any water supply to the glasshouse should be properly insulated to prevent the pipes freezing in winter. Water pipes to unheated glasshouses should be drained in winter to prevent their bursting. Even when mains water is supplied the provision of a water butt to store rainwater from the roof is a great boon, as some ericaceous plants, such as azaleas, prefer soft water. It is a good idea for any such store to be kept inside the glasshouse as no plant will benefit from freezing cold water. Sink a galvanized or plastic water tank in the ground under the glasshouse bench, and supply it with rainwater from the roof by diverting the downpipe from the guttering through the side of the glasshouse into the tank. An overflow should be fitted to the top of the tank to drain away excess water once the tank is full. It is advisable to cover any tanks to keep out insects and avoid accidents with children. Although some glasshouses are supplied with guttering and downpipes, on cheaper models they may come as optional extras.

Electricity

Even the unheated glasshouse will benefit from the provision of electricity. It is needed for accurate environmental controls and is the only source of power for mist propagators and soil-heating cables. For those who work in their glasshouses during the dark winter evenings, electric lighting is essential. It is very important that all electrical appliances used in the glasshouse are approved for such use, are installed by a qualified electrician, and are operated in accordance with their instructions. It is very dangerous to use unprotected electrical equipment within the damp environment of a glasshouse. A residual current device (RCD) will need to be fitted by a qualified electrician to guard against

electric shocks. Before installing a supply to a glasshouse an electrician will need to know what electrical items will be used so that a sufficiently large cable can be supplied.

Natural gas

Where an electricity supply is unavailable or if natural gas turns out to be the cheaper fuel, it may be worth installing a gas main if the glasshouse is situated near to the house or not too far away from an existing supply. Installation of a gas supply should only be carried out by a properly trained person authorized by the gas supply company. The high cost of installing a gas supply is the main reason for many people opting for bottled gas (see page 26). Only gas heaters intended for glasshouses should be used as these are designed so that few toxic gases are given off.

It pays in the long term to equip a glasshouse properly from the outset. The attractive brick path is easy to sweep clean and an ideal surface for damping down, while a tap inside the glasshouse makes watering a much easier task.

Heating

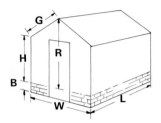

L= Length of glasshouse
   2.5m

W=Width of glasshouse
   1.8m

R= Height of glass to
   ridge 1.3m

H= Height of glass to
   eaves 0.7m

G= Roof slope 1.2m

B= Height of brick walls
   0.8m

Before installing a glasshouse heating system, you need to decide which plants you wish to grow so that a minimum growing temperature for them can be calculated (see chart below). Once this has been determined, you can make an informed decision about which system to buy. This is done by working out your heating requirement (see below), which is expressed either in kilowatts (kW), or, less often, British Thermal Units (Btu) per hour. The output of any heater, printed on the equipment or supplied with it, is expressed in the same way.

One of the most valuable tools for the glasshouse gardener is a thermometer. A maximum/minimum thermometer will give a good indication of temperature fluctuations and is essential for checking whether the glasshouse is properly ventilated during the day and heated at night. Traditional mercury and alcohol thermometers are cheaper than but not so accurate as the battery-operated digital models. Take readings by placing the thermometer among the plants, away from direct sunlight.

Equipment

It is always a good idea when installing anything but the simplest heating system to consult a heating engineer who will be able to advise on the model and size of system required and the costs involved.

Electric heaters

For the small glasshouse owner electricity offers the most versatile heating option. It is clean, trouble-free and easily controlled and, because it provides heat only when it is required, it can work out to be the most cost-efficient. Only use heaters that are designed and approved for glasshouses.

There are two main types of electric heater on the market – tubular and fan. Tubular heaters are four times as expensive as fan heaters and may be supplied without the required safety guards or thermostats. With these extras, a tubular heater could cost seven times as much as a fan heater.

In contrast, most fan heaters are supplied with a thermostat that reacts to the cool air being drawn into the heater. The thermostatic controls are generally not marked off in degrees so they need to be adjusted over a few days for the required temperature to be maintained. A fan heater works by sucking in cool air which is then drawn over heating elements and expelled to circulate around the glasshouse. With some models the fan is independent from the heater and can continue running after the heater has

Calculating heating needs

The diagram above illustrates a typical glasshouse and gives the measurements on which the calculation of heating requirements is based. The chart below gives an idea of cost in relation to temperature.

The following calculation is for a traditional, single-glazed glasshouse. If the glasshouse is double- or triple-glazed with sealed glass or plastic panels, the heat loss figure can be reduced by half. Where other glazing materials are used, the supplier should be able to give accurate heat loss figures for their structures.

To work out the heating requirement, first take the following measurements:

Minimum winter temperature	Conditions	Cost
4°C (40°F)	Frost-free	a*
10°C (50°F)	Temperate	a × 2
15°C (60°F)	Tropical	a × 5

*a=minimum cost of providing frost-free conditions. The cost of maintaining higher temperatures is calculated approximately in multiples of the basic cost.

● Equivalent surface area. This is calculated by adding together the inside surface area of the glass walls, roof slope and gable ends and half the surface area of the dwarf brick walls (brick walls lose approximately half as much heat as glass).

● Temperature lift. This is the maximum normal temperature difference required between the inside and outside of the glasshouse. To be as accurate as possible, the outside temperature you use should be the average lowest temperature over 20 years, taken from local meteorological records.

The calculation is then as follows:

cut out. This helps to maintain good air circulation and even temperatures throughout the glasshouse.

Paraffin heaters

Paraffin heaters provide the most basic form of heating and are suitable only for the smallest of glasshouses. They are easy to install and portable, as well as cheap to buy and run. However, there is no thermostatic control, which results in fluctuating temperatures making this form of heating suitable only as a back-up heat source or where no more than a 6°C (43°F) temperature rise is required. If a greater temperature rise is needed, the concentration of harmful gases that this could create may damage the plants. In addition, the fumes given off by paraffin will increase humidity and condensation, encouraging fungal diseases like grey mould (*Botrytis*). If you do use a paraffin heater, it is a good idea to ventilate the glasshouse at least once a day. Always use blue-flame heaters and set the wick correctly to keep harmful gases to a minimum.

Paraffin heaters require regular maintenance. The wick needs to be trimmed to ensure efficient burning, and the fuel needs topping up at least daily. If it is allowed to run dry, the wick will smoulder creating soot, and toxic gases will be given off. The

economy of installation and lower fuel costs of paraffin heaters are soon outweighed by their inefficiency and inconvenience.

Gas heaters

Natural gas (where available) is a cheap source of heat that can be used without a flue. Thermostats are included on some gas heaters, although they frequently need calibrating with an accurate thermometer to make sure that they run correctly. The

Fan heaters are simple to install and an efficient means of controlling the glasshouse temperature. They also ensure good air circulation which helps to reduce the spread of fungal disease in winter.

$$\text{Heating required (kW)} = \frac{8 \times \text{Equivalent surface area (m}^2) \times \text{Temperature lift (}^\circ\text{C)}}{1000}$$

[Heating required (Btu/hour) =
1.4 × Equivalent surface area (sq ft) × Temperature lift (°F)]

Example:
If your glasshouse is situated in an area where the minimum winter temperature is −7°C, and you wish to grow *Clianthus puniceus*, which likes a frost-free glasshouse with an ideal minimum winter temperature of 4°C, the temperature lift is 11°C.

To calculate the equivalent surface area of the glasshouse illustrated opposite, make the following calculation:

Surface area of glass walls and roof slope
2 × (H + G) × L = 2 × (0.7m + 1.2m) × 2.5m
= 9.5m²
Surface area of gable ends
(R + H) × W = (1.3m + 0.7m) × 1.8m
= 3.6m²
Half surface area of brick wall
(L + W) × B = (2.5m + 1.8m) × 0.8m
= 3.4m²
Add these three figures together
9.5 + 3.6 + 3.4 = 16.5m²

$$\text{Heating required (kW)} = \frac{8 \times 16.5 \times 11}{1000}$$
= 1.452kW

Round your final figure up to the nearest .5kW. You will then need to add an additional 25 per cent to the calculated heating requirement to ensure that the heater you choose will be able to cope with any sudden demands in heat and make up any shortfall between the stated and actual heat output. This glasshouse will therefore need a heater with an output of 1.9kW which is best supplied by a small fan heater, available in outputs of 2 and 3kW.

Cacti and other succulents require light and airy conditions and will develop corky lesions if kept in too warm and humid an environment during winter. If paraffin or gas heaters are used, regular ventilation will be necessary to dissipate the excess water vapour.

attached to the outside of the cylinder, the only way of checking how much gas remains is to rock the cylinder. The most fail-safe method of this form of heating is to have a switch-over valve that allows the back-up cylinder to take over when the first runs out. Propane is the best gas to use because it produces fewer toxic fumes, but if good ventilation is not provided, the fumes which are produced could cause leaf edges to brown and leaves to drop.

Hot water heaters

Hot water pipes running around the inside walls and heated by solid fuel or oil-fired boilers are ideal where high temperatures need to be maintained or for larger glasshouses where a great output of heat is needed. The simplest solid fuel boilers give little or no automatic control over heat in the glasshouse and can involve some considerable work keeping them stocked with fuel and removing ashes. Modern oil-fired boilers will provide accurate and efficient heating controls. To provide more space in the glasshouse these boilers should be sited outside. Where heating pipes are placed below benching, a gap should be left between the bench and the side wall of the glasshouse. This allows the free circulation of air and prevents cold spots.

Where the glasshouse is adjacent to the house, it is quite effective to install radiators in the glasshouse and run them off the house boiler as long as there is sufficient boiler capacity. To ensure that the glasshouse heating does not turn off when the household heating shuts down at night, a separate, thermostatically-controlled feed from the boiler will allow it to run independently.

Hot air heaters

Systems using piped hot water have a high installation cost and, for this reason alone, many growers who have large glasshouses opt for hot air boilers. These are situated inside the glasshouse, ideally on the sunless side to prevent casting shadows on the plants. A flue passing through the roof should be placed so that prevailing winds carry the flue deposits away from the glasshouse. To provide efficient heat distribution, the warm air should be channelled through polythene tubes.

heater selected should be approved for glasshouse use and fitted by a qualified gas fitter. Natural gas consists mostly of methane which when burnt produces small quantities of toxic gases that can cause leaf or bud drop. It is for this reason that adequate ventilation should always be provided. Installing a new gas supply to a glasshouse distant from the house can be expensive, and this is when bottled gas should be considered.

Although bottled gas is, in itself, expensive when compared with natural gas, it is convenient where a piped supply is unavailable. A deposit is often required on the cylinders and it is always a good idea to have a spare. The cylinders should be positioned on a firm standing area just outside the glasshouse. Unless you fit a pressure valve, which can be expensive, or a liquid crystal indicator which is

Heat conservation

Having decided which heating system to buy, you should then consider how to reduce your heating costs by limiting the amount of heat that is lost. This can be achieved by insulating the inside of the glasshouse with materials that are poor heat conductors, sealing any gaps or holes and altering crop management (see page 28).

Insulation

Double-glazed structures are the most efficient in terms of heat conservation. The most expensive, and probably the best, are the sealed, double glass panels that provide good insulation and light transmission. However, these panels are heavy and require substantial support if they are to be used in glasshouse roofs. A compromise is to use them in the sides of the glasshouse for aesthetic and structural reasons, and lighter, double thickness polycarbonate sheets in the roof. It is important that any cut ends of polycarbonate are sealed with waterproof tape to prevent condensation forming between the two layers, as this will cut out a lot of light.

Single-glazed structures can be insulated cheaply by attaching an internal skin of polythene to the inside of the glasshouse. This will give the best light transmission but a maximum heat saving of only 30 per cent. Only use polythenes intended for glasshouse use as they contain UV inhibitors that keep the polythene in good condition for up to three years.

Although more expensive than a single layer of polythene, bubble polythene incorporating two layers gives a heat saving of 40 per cent, and bubble polythene with larger bubbles and three layers a saving of 47 per cent. However, each layer will reduce light in the glasshouse by between 10–14 per cent, making a total reduction in light levels of as much as 42 per cent for bubble insulation incorporating three layers of polythene. A compromise has to be found between the benefits of reduced heating bills and the decrease in plant quality caused by insufficient light. For this reason I would recommend insulating with double thickness bubble polythene. However, it should be left off the sunny side of the glasshouse to make the most of the winter sun if light-demanding winter crops, such as calceolarias and lettuce, are grown.

It is important that insulating sheets are fixed firmly to prevent sagging, approximately 60cm (2ft) apart on the glazing bars and at each change of angle in the glasshouse. A 2.5cm (1in) gap should be allowed between the glass and the polythene to get full benefit from the insulation. In wooden glasshouses the polythene sheeting may be attached to the underside of the glazing bars with drawing pins or double-sided waterproof tape. On aluminium alloy glasshouses insulating plugs can be pushed and secured into a slot on the inside of the glazing bar, and extenders provide the required gap between the glass and polythene. At the corners of the glasshouse, where ordinary plugs may not fit, special angled clips are available that fit many glasshouses, otherwise use double-sided sticky pads. On steel houses there are no slots on the glazing bars and few useful attachment points, so the insulation should be fixed using double-sided waterproof tape. Alternatively, wooden battens may be bolted to the glazing bars and polythene fixed as for wooden houses.

Instead of using insulating plugs, you could drape the polythene sheets over tensioned wires running along the inside eaves and ridge. The advantage of this method is that it makes the rolling up and removal of the polythene easier, but the disadvantage is that the polythene is less firmly secured and therefore more likely to sag.

The best time to insulate your glasshouse is in late summer after emptying it and thoroughly washing it down with a proprietary glasshouse cleaner. Care must be taken to ensure that any moss caught between the glazing bars and glass is removed. In my experience a motorized pressure washer is a good tool for this job, although a bucket of warm, soapy water and a scrubbing brush will suffice. You should also replace any broken or cracked panes of glass and check that all the panes are fitting properly.

Fittonia verschaffeltii var. *argyroneura* 'Minima'
This attractive foliage plant for the tropical glasshouse has small, ovate, mid-green leaves highlighted with a net of silver veins, hence its common name of silver net leaf. Sensitive to the cold and draughts, its leaves will quickly shrivel if temperatures drop below 15°C (60°F).

Temperate and tropical plants such as the ferns Adiantum raddianum, Platycerium bifurcatum, Drynaria quercifolium *and the climber* Hoya motoskei *are expensive to look after in winter unless the glasshouse is properly insulated to keep down heating costs.*

Taking measurements

When calculating how much polythene to buy, you should measure the interior length of the glasshouse to work out how many widths of polythene are required to insulate the complete run of the house, allowing a 10cm (4in) overlap between sheets. The length of each section of polythene is calculated by measuring the height of a side, and the distance between the roof eaves and ridge. These two figures are then added together and multiplied by two. Ends and doors have to be made to measure, although an insulating curtain of polythene can be secured above the inside of the door to prevent sudden heat loss when the door is opened. Remember that insulation covering ventilators and louvres will need to be cut on three sides so that they can be opened on sunny days. The polythene is then secured back by clips or double-sided sticky pads.

Netting materials, which are used to provide shading in summer, can provide some insulation in winter. However, as insulating materials they are not as effective as polythene because they cast too much shade. Where forced air ventilation is used, large, reinforced flexible plastic sheets can be draped permanently over the top of the entire glasshouse,

and secured with wires or cord. Where top vents are in operation, the plastic should be secured on each side of the roof below the top vent. The sheets are cloudy, though, and therefore decrease light transmission, but, in their favour, there is a reduction in heat loss as all cracks and holes are covered. Their greatest advantage, I believe, is that they keep the glass and glazing bars dry, preventing the growth of moss, and so there are fewer problems with internal drips splashing delicate seedlings and cuttings.

Crop management

You can also save on heating costs by managing your plants in a cost-effective way. If the glasshouse contains some plants that require a higher temperature than others, group the heat-demanding plants at one end of the glasshouse, separating them with a polythene curtain. For a more permanent solution many manufacturers offer glazed divisions to section off their glasshouses.

Where glasshouses are used mainly for spring propagation, a large, heated propagator will allow the early sowing of plants while the glasshouse is kept just frost-free allowing tender plants to remain dormant during the winter.

SAVING HEAT

As well as insulating your glasshouse, you can help to conserve heat in a number of other ways. The more of the following points that can be carried out, the greater the savings on heating. However, if only a few can be put into practice, it will still be worthwhile.

● The glasshouse should be sited away from frost hollows and cold winds which put a heavy burden on any heating system (see page 19).

● Seal up any holes or cracks in the glasshouse with a mastic sealant. A clear silicon lap sealant may also be used to seal the gaps between panes.

● Fit exterior roller shading which, when lowered at night, will reduce heat loss by acting as a thermal blanket.

● Use economy electrical meters (if available) which charge less than the standard rate for night use. They are ideal where the maximum energy demand is at night.

● Fit a re-circulation fan with ducting which will recycle the warm air that gathers below the glasshouse roof down to plant level where it is required.

Ventilation

Whereas heat loss in winter is a problem, in summer it can be a positive advantage when glasshouse temperatures soar considerably above outside temperatures. Ventilation is then required to keep the temperatures down to a level at which plants can thrive, and to remove the still, humid air which encourages the development of diseases. You can achieve this in two ways – by natural ventilation where warm air escapes and cool air enters through vents in the glasshouse roof (ridge vents), or by forced air ventilation where motorized fans designed specifically for glasshouses suck warm air out of the glasshouse, pulling cool air in through openings on the opposite side.

If cooling by natural ventilation, make sure you do not underestimate the number of ridge ventilators you need. As a rule of thumb, an area equivalent to 16–20 per cent of the ground area of the glasshouse should be allocated as a minimum in ridge ventilator area (see chart). Ridge ventilators should open up to an angle of 50 degrees.

The addition of side vents, which are optional extras on many small glasshouses, will provide a more rapid movement of air. Cool air is drawn in from the side vents and as it heats up it rises until it is drawn out of the ridge vents. If only top ventilation is fitted, take care not to open the vents too rapidly as on cold days rising warm air will be replaced by a block of cold air which can prove a shock to plants.

Where additional vents are available, the best combination is alternate ridge vents and louvres on the side walls. Louvres will give adequate side ventilation and are less likely to cause draughts than standard ventilators. The door opening can provide additional ventilation, which is particularly valuable in small glasshouses, but this is not always desirable where security is a problem. Ventilators should be provided on all sides of the glasshouse so that on windy days the windward side can be closed to prevent draughts, while ventilation is open on the leeward side.

Most small glasshouses are supplied with a manual pin-and-stay method of securing the ventilators. Frequently the supplied stays are too short, allowing only a small ventilator opening, and, if this is the case, longer stays should be fitted. However, in small glasshouses the temperature can rise rapidly and, unless continually monitored, manual control will lead to wide fluctuations in temperature. For this reason I would recommend some form of automatic opening system.

Air flow with ventilation

Sufficient ventilation in the glasshouse is essential for healthy plant growth. Warm air gathering inside the roof is released through the ridge vents to be replaced by cooler air. Side vents or louvres increase the air flow still further by drawing in cool air as the rising warm air escapes through the ridge vents.

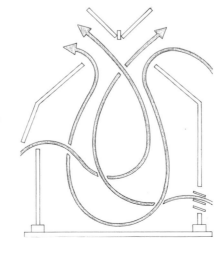

Calculating ventilation needs			
Glasshouse size	Ground area	Ridge ventilator space required (20% of ground area)	Number of 0.6 × 0.6m (2 × 2ft) ridge vents required
1.8 × 2.5m (6 × 8ft)	4.5m² (48sq ft)	0.9m² (9½sq ft)	3
2.5 × 3m (8 × 10ft)	7.5m² (80sq ft)	1.5m² (16sq ft)	4
3 × 3.7m (10 × 12ft)	11.1m² (120sq ft)	2.2m² (24sq ft)	6
3.7 × 4.3m (12 × 14ft)	15.9m² (168sq ft)	3.2m² (33½sq ft)	9

Many flowering plants, such as Celosia plumosa *and* Cleome spinosa, *fade in summer if the glasshouse becomes too hot. An efficient ventilation system, with continuous roof vents providing the maximum roof opening, is essential.*

weight of conventional ventilator mechanisms. The fans should be made specifically for glasshouse use and be able to move large volumes of air at slow speeds to avoid creating draughts.

Fans are usually placed high up in small glasshouses, often at the gable-ends, and should be shuttered to prevent cool air blowing through when the fan is inoperative. The major disadvantage of forced air ventilation is that it is noisy, totally reliant on electricity with no emergency manual override, and expensive to run. On hot days the fan will have to run continually and in the event of a power cut the glasshouse will overheat with possibly disastrous consequences. The system costs more to run than an automated natural ventilation system and, except where extra cooling is required, is no better.

Humidity

Ventilation is also used to maintain the required humidity. As the temperature rises, humidity (measured as a percentage of water vapour in the air) will decrease. If the air becomes too dry, young plants with soft foliage and some large-leaved foliage plants may desiccate and become scorched at the leaf margins. Plants lose moisture through pores in their leaves – a process known as transpiration. The water loss increases as humidity decreases, which explains why plants require more watering during warm, sunny weather. Young plants desiccate easily because their soft leaves lose more moisture than can be taken up by the developing root systems. It is therefore most important to acclimatize young plants slowly to drier conditions, whether it be from the propagator to the glasshouse bench, or from the glasshouse to the garden (see pages 45 and 61).

Humidity is increased by damping the glasshouse floor and benches, and is required in summer at least two or three times a day. In winter when temperatures are low, humidity is high, resulting in a slow transpiration rate. This can be increased by improving the air circulation and reducing the humidity by ventilating when temperatures allow. Humidity is measured with a hydrometer. Small meters in the form of a dial or digital read-out are available for the small glasshouse gardener and will give a reasonable indication of humidity.

Cheap and reliable automatic vent openers are available for hinged and louvred ventilators; these require no electricity to operate nor any maintenance. They are operated by a temperature-sensitive ram that expands with heat, opening the vent, and contracts as it cools, closing the vent. They are adjustable and some models can be set to start opening anywhere between 13–25°C (55–77°F).

For the small glasshouse I would recommend simple, automatic controls which will create ideal conditions for your plants and ensure that ventilation is provided only when required. This prevents the rapid fluctuations in temperature and higher fuel bills that can occur with manual control.

Forced air ventilation

Fans are often used as a means of forced air ventilation when the glasshouse is equipped with insufficient natural ventilation or when it will not take the

Shading

The main reason for shading a glasshouse is to lower the internal temperature by reducing the amount of sun that penetrates the glasshouse. On hot, sunny days, light-demanding plants, such as tomatoes, need little shading and ventilation, whereas shade-loving plants, like begonias, require up to 70 per cent shade to prevent them from overheating and scorching. If grown in too much light, many large-leaved foliage plants, such as dieffenbachias, will produce smaller, thicker leaves. Seedlings and newly-rooted cuttings require shading, as even with good ventilation the heat of the sun can desiccate sensitive leaves.

Exterior blinds

The most effective form of shading should reduce the sun's intensity before it can warm the glasshouse. This is best achieved by placing a shading material on a support 30cm (1ft) above the roof to allow good air circulation. In Victorian conservatories wooden lath blinds were used which could be rolled down to protect plants in bright conditions and then rolled up in dull weather. Wooden slatted blinds are still available, although expensive, and are one of the best forms of shading. Other types of exterior roller blinds are made of synthetic shade cloth or shaped plastic reeds linked by nylon thread. Although not as attractive as wooden slats, they achieve the same result at a lower cost.

Shading paints

Where blinds are too expensive or difficult to fit, shading paints will give good sun protection, if applied in early spring. These white paints, suitable for glass and plastic, are supplied in concentrated form and need diluting by volume (as instructed on the container) before use. Once diluted the paint is either lightly sprayed or applied with a long-handled brush on to the glass, and as it requires a few hours to dry and harden, it should be applied on days when there is little risk of rain. After hardening the paint is rain-fast but will become almost translucent when wet, letting in more light on rainy days.

In autumn, when the sun has lost its intensity, the shade paint should be removed. This can be done in stages, starting with the shady side in early autumn and finishing off with the sunny side two weeks later. Removal is easy – it can be rubbed off either with a dry cloth or a brush and water. Combine this task with a general autumn clean-up of the glasshouse.

Interior blinds

Interior shading will reduce sun glare on the plants but is not as effective at reducing temperatures as exterior blinds. A wide range of materials is available for interior glasshouse shading. Simple and inexpensive green shade cloth from garden centres is perfectly adequate for a small glasshouse, or if you would like something more decorative for your conservatory, you could try venetian or hardwood cane blinds from an interior design shop. Shading materials suitable for the home are not suitable for the humid atmosphere of a glasshouse, as they will soon become mouldy and rot. If considering coloured materials, remember that they are likely to fade rapidly in a bright glasshouse.

White shading paints applied to the exterior of the glasshouse help to keep the interior cool and prevent sensitive plants from being scorched by the direct rays of the sun.

Staging

Staging is made up of purpose-built benches or tables and is important for growing plants as it lifts them off the ground, frequently the coldest part of the glasshouse. Most staging is set at a height of 75cm (2½ft), which is ideal for maintaining and observing plants, and also easier on the back!

It is helpful to know how the glasshouse will be used in order to decide on the type of staging required. If tall crops such as tomatoes are grown, the full height of the glasshouse, at least on one side, will be needed in summer. In this case, permanent staging could be provided on one side and a movable or folding bench on the sunny side, where the tomatoes are to be grown.

Many cacti or bulbous plants like their pots buried in sand, so a sturdy bench will be required to take the combined weights. Even pots and types of compost can make a difference to the weight exerted on a bench. Plants grown in soil-based composts in clay pots will be significantly heavier than those in soilless mixes and plastic pots. Where benching is intended for heavy use, it is worth checking with the manufacturer that it will be strong enough. This is especially important where the staging is supported on one side by glazing bars.

If the staging is intended mainly for the display of plants, it should be aesthetically pleasing and not detract from the plants by its unsympathetic appearance. For this reason I like traditional wooden or cast-iron staging, which may be solid, with plants sitting on a layer of gravel, or slatted, which allows better air circulation but does entail more frequent watering. Where a glasshouse has a back wall, tiered staging makes maximum use of the additional height and is a good display feature.

The most attractive Victorian or pseudo-Victorian staging is purpose-built, tiered, made of cast- or wrought-iron, painted green or white to prevent rusting, and topped with a slatted wooden or solid marble top. In one conservatory I visited, the owner had bought an old cast-iron sewing machine base and fitted a slatted top made of western red cedar. The bench then served as a garden table in summer and glasshouse staging for flowering pot plants for the rest of the year. For the working glasshouse, however, western red cedar staging is an expensive luxury – expanded galvanized steel sheets in the form of a mesh (or other materials as described below) will make a perfectly adequate bench top.

Staging materials

Although purpose-built staging can be bought from garden centres or glasshouse suppliers, it is easy to make yourself. The final cost depends upon the quality of the material used and it is often more economical to buy purpose-built staging where second-hand materials are not available.

Corrugated concrete board is the cheapest and most robust material for a solid bench top. It can be topped off with gravel to improve its appearance and help raise the humidity around the plants. The corrugation allows good drainage and strengthens the board, which is usually supported on an aluminium or brick framework.

Wood is an adaptable and attractive staging material for both the top and the supports. Use

Narrow lightweight shelves secured to the glazing bars are suitable for small potted plants such as pelargoniums. However, free-standing staging is necessary for larger and heavier plants.

Brick or reinforced concrete staging should be considered when strength and stability are needed, for example when the bench is topped with gravel or is supporting large plants in clay pots.

western red cedar or softwood that has been treated against decay with a preservative coating.

Steel will rust unless it is stainless, galvanized or properly treated with a primer and undercoat. Galvanized steel is considerably heavier than aluminium but generally trouble-free. However, if it is drilled or cut, the surface will require rust protection. Avoid using aluminium bolts as they will eventually corrode the galvanized surface. Steel can make up the whole staging, for example, a corrugated galvanized top and framework, or provide a strong framework for a wooden slatted top.

Plastic-coated steel is easy to clean and trouble-free for the first few years, after which the plastic frequently hardens and cracks in the sun, allowing the metal to rust. In my opinion it is the least attractive of the staging materials, but it can be used for both the top and supports.

Aluminium staging is often made up from angled sections which are bolted together. It is maintenance-free, lightweight and, if large sections are used, can support heavy weights. Some aluminium is covered with a powder coating, producing a hard, resistant finish.

Plastic is available for either slatted or solid bench tops. After three or four years the plastic will become brittle and break easily, and therefore is not suitable for heavy weights.

If the glasshouse is glazed to the ground, the space under the bench may be used for plants requiring less light and cooler conditions. Plants grown under the bench need to be turned weekly, otherwise they will grow towards the light and become lopsided. In half-glazed glasshouses the under-bench space can be used for storage, but do not let it become a dumping ground where pests and diseases could flourish.

Watering systems

Watering is one of the most skilled operations in the glasshouse as the requirements for each plant have to be assessed individually. There are many methods of getting the water to the plant – from a simple, long spouted watering can or garden hose with its various attachments to a host of automatic watering devices.

Hand watering

Watering cans come in many shapes and sizes, made of either galvanized metal or plastic. Capacities range from 2.25–9 litres (½–2 gallons) and it is important to select one that you can lift easily when it is full of water. A can with a long spout is best as it will allow easier control over the flow of water. A rose fitted on to the spout of a can will create a fine spray for watering delicate seedlings. A small, round rose is most suitable for watering single pots and small seedlings with minimal disturbance, while a larger, oval rose with its greater output is suitable for watering trays of pricked out seedlings and numerous pots of young plants.

Hose pipes can be fitted with a lance which often incorporates a trigger to control water flow. Lances can also be fitted with a wide range of attachments, from a mist nozzle to a coarse rose.

Automatic watering

When looking for an automatic watering system, it is preferable if the selected system can give some plants on a bench more water than others. This is because in most small glasshouses there is a wide variety of plants grown, often in different-sized pots. The systems I mention here are comparable in price although prices do start to vary with the complexity of the automation.

Capillary matting

Capillary matting is the simplest and most widely used method of watering. It comprises a synthetic water-absorbent mat which, if rolled out on a flat, level surface and fed with water, will remain uniformly moist. Pot plants placed on the moist matting take up water as required through the holes in the base of the pot. A good contact between the matting and the compost in the pot is therefore vital to allow the capillary action to work. Pots with deep drainage holes, such as clay pots, are not suitable as they prevent the free movement of capillary water.

The matting is kept moist by either a seep hose that is laid on the surface of the matting or by placing one end of the matting in a reservoir of

Automatic watering systems

● Capillary matting is the cheapest solution to the problem of holiday watering. Lay the matting on a firm, level bench covered with polythene sheeting and hang one edge in a water reservoir, such as a gutter, to keep it uniformly moist (see 1, right). ● Drip tubes are particularly useful for watering pots of assorted sizes containing a variety of different plants. Insert more drip tubes around the edges of large pots and those containing thirsty plants (see 2, right).

1

2

Regular damping down of the tropical glasshouse creates the high humidity required by the Acalypha wilkesiana *'Macrophylla',* Maranta leuconeura leuconeura, Calathea makoyana, *and* Pisonia umbellifera *'Variegata'.*

any case, a good idea to test the system out before going away to avoid any pitfalls.

To provide a constant supply of water, a cistern attached to the mains will keep any reservoir topped up. If seep hoses are used, connect them to a water supply, which is controlled either manually by turning on a tap, or automatically by a sensor which is placed on the matting. This detects whether the capillary matting is wet or dry, and turns the water supply on or off as required.

Drip tubes

Drip tubes can be controlled automatically to give a measured amount of water to each plant and can be used for bed or pot watering. For bed watering, drip tubes or seep hoses are laid along the bed and turned on for a few hours each day. For pot watering, spaghetti drip tubes give good results, as different-sized pots can be accommodated on the same bench. Established plants in large pots will need many drip nozzles, whereas small pots will require only one.

Drip systems can be set to come on by a timer which is fitted to the mains supply. This will allow watering to take place at night during the summer when evaporation is reduced. For pot watering a more complex system is needed, incorporating a sensor that measures the rate of drying out from a wick and supplying water as necessary.

Overhead spray lines

Overhead spray lines suspended from the roof will give each plant the same amount of water. Attached to a mains supply, the system is ideal for watering young plants whose foliage does not cover the compost. The disadvantages of spray lines are that in winter the foliage is kept wet, encouraging fungal disorders and, if spray lines become blocked, the plants are underwatered. However, they can be used effectively in summer to raise the humidity in the glasshouse by being placed under the bench to damp the floor. They can be controlled manually by the turn of a tap or operated on a time switch or electrical sensor.

water. The latter is most useful for holiday watering. The moist fertile conditions on the matting are ideal for moss growth, which can be scraped off but usually means that you will need to replace the matting each year. Capillary matting is suitable for established plants but young seedlings and newly-potted, slow-growing plants can be overwatered using this method as the compost stays too wet.

Setting up capillary matting is quite straightfor-ward. Attach a gutter to one side of the bench and fill with water. Then lay a sheet of polythene over the bench. Position the capillary matting so that one end lies in the water-filled gutter. If the matting is to be used while you are away on holiday, neighbours could be asked to keep the reservoir filled, or alternatively you could fit a larger reservoir. It is, in

RUNNING YOUR GLASSHOUSE

Once the glasshouse is built and the required systems and services installed, the enjoyment of glasshouse gardening can be realized to its full extent. One of its greatest pleasures is propagating your own plants and watching them develop and grow to maturity. In this chapter the equipment and techniques needed to raise plants under glass and the different methods of combating the most frequently encountered pests and diseases are discussed in detail.

Much can be achieved with careful organization in a small glasshouse. With secondary high-level staging, growing space can be increased by up to one third. Here, waist- and eye-level benching is used for growing bedding plants, such as gazanias and pelargoniums, and tender exotics, such as Zantedeschia elliottiana.

Containers

All glasshouse plants will need some kind of container unless they are grown in the glasshouse border. From shallow trays for sowing seed or planting cuttings, to huge, ornamental clay planters for summer bedding displays, there are containers for every stage of plant growth.

Trays and pots

The large surface area of trays makes them particularly suitable for sowing seed, rooting cuttings in large numbers and pricking out. Pots, on the other hand, are used primarily for growing on, although small-sized pots and shallow pans are equally useful for propagation where small numbers of plants are required.

Trays come in a wide variety of materials and sizes. The following chart illustrates the most popular types used for propagation and sets out the advantages and disadvantages of each to help you make the right selection.

Pots are also made from a number of different materials. For propagation and growing on, I prefer to use plastic pots, but if you have always used clay and get the results you want, there is no reason to change. I would, though, warn against mixing clay and plastic pots for growing small plants. This makes watering difficult and time-consuming as the plants in the porous clay pots will dry out more quickly and need more attention. Pots are measured by their diameter at the rim.

TRAYS

Material	Durability	Description and uses	Points to consider
Peat inserts	Disposable	Divided into as many as 40 units which fit into a standard-sized seed tray (38 × 23cm/15 × 9in). Ideal for space-sowing or single cuttings.	Minimal root disturbance when potting up as inserts are not removed. Must be kept moist so roots can penetrate the peat. Can be used once only. Easily damaged
Thin plastic inserts	Semi-disposable	Made in multiple units (2–48) to fit a standard-sized seed tray (see above). Ideal for all stages in the propagation of bedding plants.	Can be used for more than one season if handled with care. Must be removed before potting. Careful watering essential as it is easy to miss small units and overwater others.
Cellular	Semi-disposable	Made in a variety of plastic materials and in various sizes. Use for space-sowing seed and rooting cuttings.	As for thin plastic inserts.
Polystyrene	Semi-disposable	Usually made of 4 units joined by tape. Single unit measures approx. 20 × 5 × 5cm (8 × 2 × 2in). Use for sowing, pricking out and raising cuttings.	Can be used for more than one season. Retain heat well, keeping roots warm. More robust than plastic inserts.
Wooden trays (slats of wood are nailed together and treated with a safe wood preservative)	Long-life	Home-made to any size. Use deep trays for rooting cuttings or large seed that will be in the tray for some time, and for pricking out bedding plants. Use shallow trays for sowing seed which require little compost.	Made to measure. Heavy and bulky and difficult to store. Difficult to clean. Provide poor drainage. Absorb moisture which escalates decay. Harbour pests and diseases.
Rigid plastic	Long-Life	Deep (approx. 35 × 23 × 8cm/ 14 × 9 × 3in) and shallow (approx. 35 × 23 × 5cm/14 × 9 × 2in) trays available. For uses, see under Wooden trays.	Good quality trays will last many seasons. Easy to clean. Do not harbour pests and diseases. Easy to store.

POTS

Material	Durability	Description and uses	Points to consider
Paper	Disposable	Available up to 15cm (6in) in diameter. Ideal for quick-growing bedding plants.	Will last 10–12 weeks if kept moist. Do not remove pot at planting unless dried out.
Peat	Disposable	Use small sizes as propagation cells; medium sizes for potting up bedding plants; large sizes as patio planters.	Can be planted out with plant if kept moist so that roots penetrate the peat.
		Peat pellets are dried compressed medallions of peat that swell when soaked in water. Ideal for single large seeds or cuttings.	The thin net around the peat pellet allows good root growth and causes minimal root damage when potted on.
		Peat blocks are home-made with a blocking tool from blocking compost. Ideal for sowing seed or inserting cuttings.	Do not allow to dry out. Reduce this risk by placing blocks close to each other. Do not remove when planting out.
Black polythene	Disposable	Available in a wide range of sizes. Ideal for quick-growing bedding plants from first potting.	Very cheap. Store flat. Flexibility makes potting and watering difficult.
Thin plastic	Semi-disposable	Useful in sizes up to 13cm (5in). Use for short-term subjects from sowing to potting on.	Rigid pots are very cheap and can be re-used if not damaged at planting.
Heavy-duty paper	Long-life	Available only in large sizes. Use for final potting of tall plants.	Treated to last a full season. Remove before potting on.
Plastic	Long-life	Available in a wide range of sizes. Ideal for propagation and growing on plants. Use shallow pans for sowing small batches of seed, rooting cuttings and pricking out.	Light. Good drainage. Easy to clean. Can be used over many years. Use with soilless composts on capillary matting.
Clay	Long-life	As for plastic. Bigger sizes are ideal for large and top-heavy plants as ornamental planters.	Use frost-resistant pots if leaving out in freezing temperatures. Very porous, and so dry out quickly.

Propagating

Propagating your own plants is extremely satisfying and can be done with very little equipment. The two methods of propagation most commonly used in glasshouse cultivation are sowing seed and taking cuttings. Plants raised from cuttings will generally mature more quickly than those from seed but they may require more attention.

A considerable amount of planning is essential if you intend using the glasshouse to produce young plants for planting out. Seed must be sown and cuttings taken at the correct time so that the plants are at the right stage in their development – neither too big nor too small – when transferred outside. Try to spread the propagation work-load over a period of time so that not all your plants require handling at the same time. Holidays should also be considered so that young plants are not left at a critical stage when you are going to be away.

Propagators

The closed environment of a propagator provides the warm, moist conditions required by germinating seedlings and newly-inserted cuttings. As young plants with inadequate root systems cannot take up enough moisture from the compost, the high humidity reduces water loss from the sensitive leaves and prevents them from wilting. Make sure that you check on the progress of your seedlings and cuttings daily and remove any diseased leaves as fungal diseases also favour these conditions.

Purpose-built propagators are widely available, from simple, clear plastic tray covers to large propagators with sliding doors and thermostatically-controlled heated bases. Both are equally effective, but the extra expense of a large propagator is only warranted if it can be filled regularly with seedlings or cuttings. Another form of propagator, usually home-made, is a closed case with wooden or brick sides and a glass or polythene top. Although these cases let in less light than clear propagators, they will produce good plants – the extra light giving only a marginal advantage to slow-rooting plants.

The cheapest propagator is the polythene tent or drape. The warm, steamy environment created by placing the tent over a heated bench, with wire hoops preventing the polythene from touching any leaves, is perfect for propagating many plants. For quick-rooting cuttings, such as fuchsias which root in two weeks in the spring, trays or pots can be covered with thin polythene which, because of its light weight, rests on the leaves without causing them any harm.

A cheap but effective way of providing a propagation environment for seed is to cover the container, after sowing, with a piece of black polythene or with a pane of glass which is then covered with a sheet of newspaper. Turn the polythene or glass over at least once a day to stop the atmosphere becoming too humid.

A disadvantage of closed propagation environments is that they need shading on sunny days to prevent the young plants from overheating, and this in turn reduces the amount of light which cuts down the rate of photosynthesis (see page 44). This does not seriously affect the propagation of many plants, but for those that would benefit from extra light at the propagation stage, such as *Cistus* species, *Lippia citriodora* and *Leptospermum scoparium*, automatic mist propagation could be used.

Propagation environments can take a variety of forms – from pots covered with a polythene bag to purpose-built plastic models with integrated heated bases – as long as they provide the plants with the required warmth and humidity.

WHY PROPAGATE YOUR OWN PLANTS?
- It saves money.
- You can grow a wider range of plants that might not be available from garden centres.
- You have control over the quality of plants grown.

This multi-dibber has been hand-made from wooden pegs attached to a board. Press the dibber 1cm (½in) into the seed compost to create evenly spaced holes for space-sowing large seeds.

PREPARING THE CONTAINER
- Overfill the container with compost and level with one edge of a flat board drawn over the top.
- Compress with a firming board until the compost is 1cm (½in) below the rim.
- Place the container on the ground and tip the watering can, fitted with a fine rose, so that the first splutters of water splash to the ground.
- Pass the can over the compost until completely wetted.
- Move the can so the last splutters do not make holes in the compost.
- Alternatively, place the container in a tray of water until the compost is thoroughly moistened.

Mist propagators

Although a worry-free form of propagator, mist units are expensive to install, and for most small glasshouse owners they are an unnecessary luxury – a closed case system is much better value for money. The theory behind mist propagation is that a heated bench keeps the rooting zone warm, promoting rapid and healthy root growth, and a fine spray of mist maintains a high humidity around the leaves, preventing wilting, as well as reducing leaf temperature. This reduces respiration in the foliage and, because no shading is necessary, maximum photosynthesis can take place. The mist nozzles are controlled by an 'electric leaf' that switches the mist off when it is wet and on when dry.

Soil-heating cables

Although portable glasshouse heaters can be put under the propagation bench and trays placed on specially adapted paraffin heaters to create a warmer rooting and germination environment, temperatures will be variable. Thermostatically-controlled soil-

Sowing methods

- There are three main methods for sowing fine and medium seed. • The first is to form a spout from the opened seed packet (see 1, right). • The second is to pour a small amount of seed into the palm of one hand (see 2, right). • The third is to place a quantity of seed in one hand and gently cup the palm so that a channel is formed (see 3, right).

1 Tap the hand holding the seed packet gently and let the seed pour out over the compost at a steady rate.

2 Take pinches of seed and sprinkle evenly over the compost, rubbing the thumb and forefinger together.

3 Tap the hand holding the seed so that the seed moves down the channel evenly and on to the compost.

heating cables, however, ensure that the rooting environment of a propagator remains warm without overheating. The cables are laid on a shallow bed of sand and then covered with a further 5cm (2in) of sand. Temperature control is provided by a rod thermostat placed on the surface of the sand or by a thermostatic probe placed in a pot of compost on the heated bench. A soil thermometer is a useful tool for testing rooting temperatures in a propagator and for calibrating thermostats operating the cables.

Heated frames

Where glasshouse space is at a premium, a garden frame heated by warming cables will provide suitable conditions for the propagation of hardy and half-hardy plants, both from seed and cuttings. If managed in the same way as a closed case, it will prove to be a useful extension to the glasshouse propagation environments.

Propagation from seed

Each plant propagated from seed is individual and there will usually be a slight variation in the appearance of seedlings of the same cultivar or variety. However, F_1 seed has been specially bred to give identical physical characteristics to each plant grown. Seed saved from F_1 plants will not give the same results; some variation in flower colour, shape or size of plant will already be apparent.

Each seed is a potential plant which requires a constant supply of moisture to break its dormancy. Plants are no different from other living things in that they need oxygen to respire. A seed-sowing compost therefore needs to contain a good balance of air and water. If you combine this with a temperature of 20°C (68°F), you have the optimum conditions for germinating the seed of many glasshouse plants. Remember, though, that under these warm, moist conditions, pests and diseases also thrive, so to give your seedlings a head start, use sterilized seed or multi-purpose compost, not garden soil or used potting compost, which will also contain weed seeds. Sterilized (more accurately partially sterilized) composts have been heated to 70–80°C (158–175°F) for 10–13 minutes to kill a large proportion of the

pests and diseases present. (Complete sterilization produces a dead soil without any beneficial micro-organisms, including those that help to make nitrogen available to the plant.)

Flowering pot plants commonly grown from seed in the glasshouse are *Primula obconica*, *Cineraria × hybrida*, *Calceolaria × herbeohybrida*, *Cyclamen persicum* cultivars and *Schizanthus pinnatus* cultivars. Seed-grown vegetables include lettuce, tomato, cucumber, pepper and aubergine.

Sowing seed

When sowing large numbers of seed, use shallow trays as the seedlings will be in the tray for only a short time before being pricked out (lifted and spaced out) into other containers. However, if small amounts of seed need sowing, use half trays, shallow pots or pans, which will take up less space. Whichever containers you decide to use, make sure they are clean and sterilize them with a proprietary sterilizer to kill off any fungal spores. Rinse the container well with clean water to remove chemical residue before putting in the compost.

It is important when sowing seed to make deliberate, steady movements as sudden jerks can result in oversowing. Large seed is best space-sown, leaving sufficient space between the seeds to allow the seedlings to develop without overcrowding.

Once the container has been filled with compost, watered and drained, sow the seed evenly and not too thickly as this will make the seedlings spindly and encourage damping off, a term used for fungal diseases that attack the seedling stem (hypocotyl) causing it to collapse and rot. You can usually sow fine seed closer together than large seed because the young seedlings from fine seed are smaller and occupy less space. For example, in a standard-sized tray, you could sow 800 dust-like begonia seeds, but no more than 40 large runner bean seeds.

If you find correct spacing at all difficult when sowing fine and medium seed, you can practise by sprinkling seed on to a piece of white paper. It is easy to see the dark seed against the light paper background, and in this way you can develop some control over spacing. If you are not confident about sowing by hand, fine and medium seed may be space-

COVERING SEED

There are a number of equally effective ways to cover seed – find the method that works best for you.

- First pass the compost through a 6mm (¼in) sieve. Then sprinkle it by hand over the seed. Some practice is needed to achieve an even covering using this method.
- Hold a 6mm (¼in) sieve filled with seed compost 40–50cm (16–20in) over the container, and shake until the covering is even.
- Sprinkle a coarse layer of grit instead of compost over seed that takes a long time to germinate to prevent the growth of weeds, mosses and liverworts. With this method you cannot see when the compost needs watering so you will have to check the weight of the container or feel beneath the grit.
- Seedlings covered with peat- or coir-based composts may lift their covering like a hat. Use vermiculite instead as the seedlings will be able to push up through it.

Efficient use of glasshouse space can be made by sowing seed in square pots. Where large numbers of different plants are grown, it is important to label each pot with the plant name and date of sowing.

seed to sand, it becomes easier to handle and the light coloured sand shows up well against the dark compost, indicating where seed has been sown. With fine seed it also helps to sieve a layer of fine compost before sowing to ensure an even surface. Fine, surface-sown seed requires even, humid conditions to make sure that the seeds germinate properly and do not desiccate. As a rule, fine seed should not be covered as the germinating seedling will not have enough energy to grow through a covering of compost.

Medium-sized seed, such as tagetes and cineraria, is sown on the surface of the seed compost, then given a covering of compost equal to the depth of the seed. The depth of soil covering is important – if it is too deep, the seed will be unable to grow through it, and if too shallow, it may dry out, preventing an even germination.

Large seed, like runner bean or cyclamen, is best space-sown in trays. Use a dibber or multi-dibber, which you can make yourself by attaching screws or small wooden pegs to the underside of your firming board, to make uniformly-spaced holes in the compost. Place a single seed into each hole and cover with a light layer of compost. The layer of compost should equal the depth of the seed.

Some fine and medium seed, such as lobelia and sweet william (*Dianthus barbatus*), may be bought in a pelleted form to aid sowing. The pellets can be space-sown, like large seed, and after contact with moist compost the hard coat of the pellets breaks down, allowing moisture to reach the seed.

Aftercare

After covering, water in the seed with a watering can and fine rose, using the method for preparing the container described on page 40. Alternatively, if fine seed is sown or there is no fine rose available, the containers can be placed in a tray of water for a couple of hours allowing the compost to absorb water without disturbing the seed.

Each pot or tray should be labelled with the name of the plant and the date of sowing. It is traditional to write the name on one side of the plant label and each stage of cultivation on the other. Use a pencil or waterproof pen.

sown using a template. Drill between 40 (5 × 8), 48 (6 × 8) or 60 (6 × 10) holes in a sheet of perspex or hardboard cut to the same size as the tray. Individual seeds, or a small pinch in the case of a very fine seed, can be pushed through each hole. Although this ensures uniform spacing in the compost, it does waste glasshouse space at this early stage of growth. However, as long as groups of seedlings are thinned out to the single best, it saves time later on as pricking out is not necessary as the seedlings are already spaced.

Fine seed, such as antirrhinum, begonia and streptocarpus, is difficult to sow evenly because the tiny seeds stick together and are not easy to see. By mixing the seed with dry, fine, silver sand (available from garden centres) in a ratio of approximately 1:10

After sowing, the containers should be placed in a warm, humid atmosphere for the seedlings to germinate. The minimum temperature required depends on the species being grown, but a propagator with its thermostat set at 20°C (68°F) is ideal for many glasshouse plants. During sunny weather the propagator should be shaded from direct sunlight to prevent overheating, and containers checked daily for drying out. If dry, they should be watered with a can and fine rose.

As soon as germination is complete, place the containers on the open bench and shade them from strong sunlight which can desiccate tender seedlings fresh from the propagator. It is while the seedlings are establishing that they are susceptible to damping off. This can be avoided by using sterilized compost, sowing thinly rather than thickly, and applying a suitable fungicidal drench (following the manufacturer's instructions) after germination.

Pricking out

The process of moving seedlings from the crowded container in which they germinate to individual pots or deeper trays where they will have enough room to develop is known as 'pricking out'. Seedlings should be pricked out as soon as they are large enough to handle, which will vary from plant to plant. Begonia and streptocarpus seedlings, for example, are too small to handle when they first germinate but can be pricked out as soon as they have formed three to four true leaves. If the seedlings are left to grow any larger, they will become overcrowded, drawn and again be susceptible to damping off. Large seedlings with long roots are also extremely difficult to handle and consequently easily damaged.

The number of seedlings you prick out depends upon the number of plants you require. As a general rule, prick out 20 per cent more seedlings than you need to allow for later losses. If there is a great variation in seedling size, grade them by pricking out the largest first and working down to the smaller seedlings. Seedlings are easily damaged and should never be handled by their delicate stems.

Healthy Ageratum *'Blue Mink' seedlings have been pricked out from the crowded tray in which they germinated to a second tray where they will have room to develop.*

How to prick out

● Prepare a deep tray or pot with potting compost (see page 40). ● Make holes for each seedling with a dibber, 2.5–5mm (1–2in) apart. ● Lift the seedlings (see 1, right).
● Discard any poorly developed or diseased seedlings. ● Plant the seedlings (see 2, right). ● Firm the compost (see 3, right).
● Mark the date of pricking out on the label.
● Water thoroughly to settle the compost and apply a suitable fungicidal drench.
● Place the containers out of direct sunlight until the seedlings have rooted.

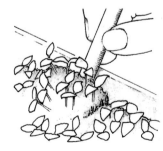

1 Lift clumps of seedlings out of the container with a dibber and separate into single seedlings.

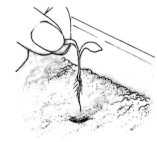

2 Hold a seed leaf between thumb and forefinger and plant so the seed leaves are just above the compost.

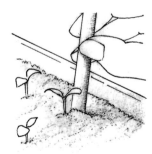

3 Firm the compost around the seedling root by inserting the dibber close to the original hole.

Propagation from cuttings

One advantage that propagation from cuttings has over seed propagation is that by removing parts of a plant and persuading them to develop into separate plants, you can produce large numbers of identical clones of the parent plant. Cuttings are used to raise a wide range of plants, typical examples of glasshouse plants being fuchsia and pelargonium cultivars, as it is possible to raise many young plants in a small space and a number of cuttings can be taken from one stock plant.

Before discussing how to propagate plants from cuttings, the roles that water, heat and light play in the process need to be understood.

Water: Water vapour is lost through the leaves of cuttings and needs to be conserved, otherwise the cuttings will wilt. But as cuttings have no roots, it is difficult for them to take up enough moisture from the rooting medium. It is therefore very important to place your cuttings in a propagation environment with a high humidity to reduce water loss (see page 39).

Heat: Most plants require a rooting temperature of 18–22°C (65–72°F). These conditions are best provided by propagators with bottom heating, unheated propagators in a warm environment or mist units (see pages 39–40).

Light: Photosynthesis is the process by which plants take in carbon dioxide and water in the presence of light to manufacture sugars which are used by the plant to provide energy for living and growing. You can influence this process by adding artificial light – fluorescent strip lights or horticultural lamps placed approximately 30cm (1ft) above the young plants – to increase day length and light intensity, or by placing cuttings in either a shady or a well-lit position, depending on the plants' needs.

Stem cuttings

Stem (shoot) cuttings may be divided into three groups – softwood, semi-ripe and hardwood – according to their age and the amount of woody tissue present. Softwood and semi-ripe cuttings are used most frequently to propagate glasshouse plants. Hardwood cuttings are taken primarily of hardy,

deciduous plants and therefore are rarely used for propagation in the glasshouse. All cuttings should be vigorous, true to type and free from any signs of pests and diseases.

Softwood cuttings These are taken from young, flexible shoot tips that are yet to form woody tissue. They can be collected all year round from some glasshouse plants, such as plectranthus and coleus, but only in spring and early summer from hardy garden plants, when there is a flush of growth. Softwood cuttings usually take 14–21 days to root. If rooting is difficult, dip the cuttings in a rooting compound (see right).

Semi-ripe cuttings These can be taken once the softwood has started to become woody, which is between mid- and late summer for deciduous plants, and late summer and early autumn for evergreens. Fuchsias, *Clianthus puniceus*, abutilons and bougainvilleas can all be raised from semi-ripe cuttings in late summer. Semi-ripe cuttings are usually taken when they are 5–15cm (2–6in) long, the actual length depending upon the plant species and amount of plant material available. For example, fuchsia cuttings are taken 8cm (3in) long and hibiscus cuttings 13cm (5in) long. Rooting compounds can be used for semi-ripe cuttings that are difficult to root (see right).

Rooting cuttings

If using rooting compound, decant a little of it into a small dish so you do not contaminate the main stock with moisture from the base of the cuttings. Then dip the base of each cutting into the compound, following the manufacturer's instructions.

Most cuttings do best if inserted in a tray or pot of moist, free-draining compost, filled using the method described earlier for seed sowing (see page 40). A basic mix that suits most plants is made up of equal parts peat and sharp sand or coir fibre and sharp sand. As these cutting mixes contain little or no fertilizer, it is important to pot the rooted cuttings up as soon as possible before they start to suffer from lack of nutrients. An 8–9cm (3–3½in) pot is adequate at this stage. If cuttings take a long time to

ROOTING COMPOUNDS
Rooting compounds are available either as powders or liquids containing plant hormones – IBA (indolebutyric acid) and NAA (naphthaleneacetic acid) being the most effective – that help to improve the formation of roots. They should be stored in a cool, dry place, such as a refrigerator, and not kept for longer than 12 months, after which time they are no longer effective. Different types of cutting require rooting compounds of different concentrations, softwood cuttings needing the lowest. Liquid preparations are diluted with water, according to the manufacturer's instructions, to suit the type of cutting, while separate powder formulations are available for all types of cutting. General powder formulations are also manufactured which are used successfully for many softwood and semi-ripe cuttings.

root, give the leaves a foliar feed to restore the nutrient balance (see page 53). Plant each cutting by making a hole with a dibber and inserting it to just below the basal leaves. After all the cuttings are inserted, water them in with a watering can and fine rose to settle the compost around the base of the cuttings. Then place the tray or pots in a propagation environment (see page 39) until roots are formed. For some plants, *Actinidia kolomikta* for example which although hardy is best propagated in the glasshouse from softwood cuttings with a heel, and the popular busy lizzie (*Impatiens*), rooting can take as little as a week.

Cuttings that form fragile root systems and resent disturbance, such as poinsettias (*Euphorbia pulcherrima*), may be inserted directly into small peat blocks or pots. When roots appear at the edge of the peat, the cuttings are ready for potting up.

Aftercare

Cuttings should be checked daily for watering and closed environments should be shaded and ventilated on sunny days to prevent overheating. Any dead or diseased foliage should be removed to prevent the development of grey mould (*Botrytis*). Once rooted, harden off the cuttings by gradually providing more ventilation until they can sit happily on the open bench. They can then be potted up as described on page 48.

Root disturbance at potting can be reduced by inserting cuttings, such as fuchsias, directly into peat pots or pellets. The plants are ready for potting up once the roots show through the peat. Renewed shoot growth is a good indication of a healthy rooting.

Preparation of cuttings

● The most common method of taking a softwood cutting is to make a clean cut just below a leaf node (where the leaf joins the stem). This is called a nodal cutting (see 1, right). ● As some plants will produce roots all along the stem, they can be cut between two nodes. This is called an internodal cutting (see 2, right). ● Semi-ripe cuttings are best obtained from lateral shoots, prepared in the same way as softwood cuttings, or taken as heel cuttings. Trim the heel before inserting into the compost (see 3, right).

1 *Cut shoots 5–10cm (2–4in) long from the tips of plants with a sharp knife and remove any lower leaves.*

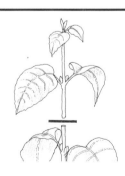

2 *Cut shoots 5–10cm (2–4in) long between two leaf nodes. This method works very well for fuchsias.*

3 *Tear a lateral shoot carefully from the mother plant, leaving a heel of older wood hanging from the base.*

Leaf cuttings

Leaf-stem (leaf-petiole) cuttings can be taken from rosetted plants with long leaf stems, such as *Peperomia caperata* and african violets (*Saintpaulia ionantha*). The leaf and stem are removed from the plant and the stem trimmed back to 4–5cm (1½–2in). The stem is then inserted at a slight angle into cutting mix, just deep enough to keep the leaf upright. Plantlets will form from the cut end and, when they have formed an adequate root system, can be separated from the mother leaf and potted up individually.

Plants with large fleshy leaves, such as *Begonia rex* cultivars and *Streptocarpus* hybrids, can be propagated from whole leaf (lamina) cuttings. Healthy, mature leaves are selected and the leaf stem removed and discarded.

The preferred method for *Begonia rex* is to lay the leaf upside down on a firm surface and sever each vein at two points along its length. The leaf is then nestled into cutting mix, with the underside of the leaf facing downward. You can weigh down the leaf with stones to help increase the contact with the compost. After some weeks young plants will develop where the cuts were made in the veins and when these plants are large enough, they can be separated and potted up.

A less common but more space-saving method is to discard the outer 2cm (¾in) of the leaf and cut the remainder into square sections, each containing a prominent vein. Insert one third of each section into the cutting compost or nestle it on top. Where a small number of quick-growing, large streptocarpus plants are required, cut a leaf into arrow-shaped sections and insert a third of each section at a 45 degree angle into the cutting mix. However, where a large number of plants are required and only a few leaves can be removed, cut a leaf from the plant and trim its tip and base before cutting out the central midrib. The cut sides of the two halves are then inserted by one third into the cutting mix. Plantlets will develop where lateral veins have contact with the compost.

Leaf-bud cuttings allow a large number of plants to be propagated from a small amount of propagation material as all that is required is a healthy leaf, bud and stem section. *Ficus elastica*, *Aphelandra squarrosa* and camellias are often propagated by this method. Select a healthy stem from the parent plant and cut it into sections just above each leaf and approximately 2.5cm (1in) below so that each cutting contains a leaf and dormant bud. Stems with opposite leaves and buds can be split even further by cutting along the length of the stem, leaving two leaf and stem sections. Insert the stem section in compost so that the leaf stem touches the surface of the compost. Leaves should be inserted facing the same direction to make the maximum use of available space and make removal after rooting easier.

***Tolmiea menziesii* 'Taff's Gold'**
Although frost-hardy, this clump-forming perennial is a popular foliage plant for hanging baskets in the cool glasshouse. Its common name is the pick-a-back plant as a young plantlet develops on each leaf. If leaves with plantlets are removed and nestled in a rooting medium, the plantlets will root and develop into new plants.

Leaf and leaf-bud cuttings

A Begonia rex *leaf is laid flat on the compost with its veins cut to encourage the formation of plantlets.*

Squares cut out of a Begonia rex *leaf, each containing a vein, are nestled into the compost at a slight angle.*

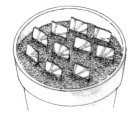

A streptocarpus leaf with its tip, base and midrib removed, is inserted cut-side in the compost.

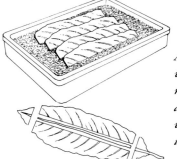

A streptocarpus leaf with its tip and base removed, is cut into arrow-shaped sections which are inserted upright into the compost.

Plants with opposite leaves can be sliced in two to make double leaf-bud sections which are inserted separately in the compost.

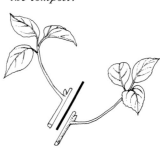

Leaf-bud cuttings of large-leaved plants, such as *Ficus elastica*, can also be inserted singly into small pots and the large leaves curled around a cane and secured with an elastic band. This will help to secure the cutting, make the most of the available space and reduce water loss from the leaf.

Plantlets

A number of plants, such as the succulent *Kalanchoe tubiflora*, produce plantlets on their leaves. These can be removed and pricked out into a pot or tray and placed in a propagator until established. Once they have formed an adequate root system, they can be potted up separately and grown on to maturity. Runners or young plantlets which form on the old flower stems of spider plants (*Chlorophytum comosum*) can also be detached from the parent plant and potted up separately.

Offsets

Buds or shoots formed under the soil with an independent root system are known as offsets or toes, and are found on mother-in-law's tongue (*Sansevieria trifasciata*), agaves, yuccas and aloes. Sever the toes from the parent plant with a knife when they have formed their own root system, and pot them up individually. Dracaenas are often lifted from their pots by the strong growth of these toes which are yet to form roots. If these rootless sections are cut off into 3cm (1¼in) long sections, potted up into 8cm (3in) pots and placed in a warm, humid position, they will soon develop roots and foliage.

The tropical foliage plant *Dieffenbachia* develops thick, leafless stems which can be sliced up into 5cm (2in) long sections. These should then be lined out in trays with their dormant buds facing uppermost and half covered with compost. They require a temperature of 22°C (72°F) and a high humidity before root and shoot development will take place. Once well established, pot them up separately.

Division

Clump-forming plants can be propagated by splitting or dividing the clump into a number of sections which are then potted up and grown on separately. Large plants, such as *Clivia miniata*, can be divided

using two garden forks which are pushed back to back into the centre of the clump. Pull the forks apart to separate the clump. Smaller plants, such as *Primula* 'Kewensis', can be divided by hand or, if stubborn, with two hand forks.

Layering

Layering is used for climbers or shrubs that are difficult to root from cuttings, such as *Lapageria rosea*. Make a cut half way into a stem of the parent plant, underneath a leaf joint, and apply rooting compound. Anchor the stem in a pot of cutting mix or the glasshouse border if that is where the parent plant is growing, and pin it down with a wire staple. Once a well-established root system has developed, cut the layer from the parent plant.

Streptocarpus, propagated from leaf cuttings taken in late winter, make most attractive flowering plants in summer. Young plants should be potted into a 9cm (3½in) pot but will need a 13cm (5in) pot before flowering.

Potting

OPPOSITE *After potting, rooted cuttings should be spaced pot-thick on the glasshouse bench to help them become established, at the same time making the best use of the available space. However, rapidly growing plants, such as* Plectranthus saccatus *var.* longitubus *and* Ruellia macrantha *shown here, will often need spacing out after only a week.*

The key to success when potting your plants is in the organization of the potting bench. A good supply of fresh potting compost should be piled up in the middle of the bench, together with enough clean pots stacked on one side and space for the potted plants on the other.

Potting up

This refers to the process of moving rooted cuttings and seedlings from their group containers to individual small pots (8–9cm/3–3½in) where the root system has more room and sufficient nutrients to expand and develop.

Foliage growth in a cutting indicates that rooting has taken place. Remove the pot to check if there are any roots showing on the outside of the rooting medium. If there are, the cutting is ready for potting up. If not, replace the cutting and check again in a few days' time. Seedlings are ready to pot up when they have filled their container and the leaves are touching. If left for too long, seedlings will become drawn, and cuttings will starve and the long roots of both will damage easily during potting. Once potted up, plants should be kept out of direct sunlight for a couple of days to prevent them from wilting and desiccating in the hot sun.

Potting on

This is the process of moving a plant that has filled its pot with roots into a larger pot with fresh potting compost. Plants first potted into an 8–9cm (3–3½in) pot should be potted on to an 11.5–13cm (4½–5in) pot to allow for further development. The ideal time to pot on a plant is when its roots have fully circled the compost in the pot but not formed a tight mat of roots. To examine the rootball, loosen the pot by tapping it on the edge of the bench, then remove the pot while supporting the rootball in the palm of the hand. The correct timing of potting does make a big difference to the quality of plants produced. If left too long, the plants will become pot-bound and short of nutrients, which can result in yellowing and loss of lower foliage. Potted on too early, before the roots have occupied the whole pot, will at best be a waste of space and compost, and at worst will lead to overwatering as the compost will stay too damp. It is important that a plant's rootball is moist before potting on otherwise it can be difficult to re-wet.

Aftercare

All newly potted plants are best placed on the glasshouse bench pot-thick, with their foliage just

---

How to pot up and pot on

Place enough potting compost in a clean pot to ensure that the top of the rootball will come approximately 2–5cm (¾–2in) below the rim, depending on the size of the pot. Hold the plant stem so that the rootball is in the middle of the pot and introduce fresh compost up to the rim. Settle soilless compost by tapping the pot on the potting bench; soil-based composts should be firmed with the index and middle fingers until the compost is 1cm (½in) below the rim. Water in with a can and fine rose.

Support the top of the rootball (above) and knock the pot against the bench to release the plant (right).

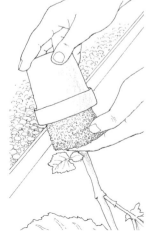

Place the plant in the centre of the new pot on a layer of fresh, lightly firmed compost.

touching. By having the plants a little closer at this stage, a microclimate is created that is more humid than if the pots are spaced further apart. Once the plants start to grow, they should regularly be given more space because if they are left to become crowded, with one plant shading another and competing for light and space, they will become drawn and more susceptible to pests and diseases. Garden plants raised under glass need to be hardened off before they can be planted outside. Do this either in a cold frame (see page 61) or a well-ventilated, unheated glasshouse.

Rejuvenating pot-bound plants

A plant is pot-bound when its root system has become tight and restricted and the roots form a compressed core at the base of the pot. Such plants will often show signs of reduced vigour with smaller, yellowing leaves. Some gardeners allow vigorous plants to become pot-bound as this will give them some control over excessive growth, but for many plants it will result in a reduced performance.

If your plants are only slightly pot-bound, remove approximately 2–3cm (¾–1¼in) of surface compost – an old plant label is a useful tool for prising compost away from the surface roots. Then top-dress the plant with some fresh compost and water in. If the plants are very pot-bound but you do not wish to pot on to a larger size, remove the pots, taking care not to damage the plants. (Unfortunately, some plants are held so firmly that their pots must be broken to release the rootball.) Use a dibber or old plant label to prise the compost away from the outside of the rootball. Select up to one third of the thickest and most vigorous roots, particularly those that are badly entwined around the base of the pot, and cut back to the rootball with a knife or secateurs. Then pot the plant back into its original container with fresh compost. This treatment can cause a shock to some established plants and they may drop their leaves. Minimize this risk by repotting in late winter when the days are getting lighter and warmer, but before any new growth takes place.

Fill the space between the rootball and the pot with compost, ensuring no gaps are left.

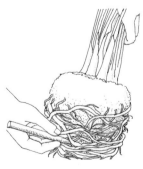

Use a dibber to loosen the roots of pot-bound plants, especially those congested at the base.

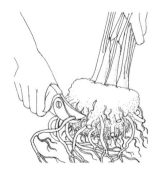

Remove one third of the thicker roots, leaving the fibrous ones that absorb most water and nutrients.

Composts

BORDER SOIL

Glasshouse crops grown in the border, such as tomatoes, require less frequent watering and feeding as their roots are unrestricted by a container. However, growing the same crops in the same border year after year causes a build-up of pests, diseases, salts and plant acids which will reduce the vigour and health of plants. This should be avoided by rotating crops and replacing the border soil with garden soil every three to four years.

The soil should first be analysed for nutrients and pH with a proprietary soil testing kit. The analysis will determine the lime and fertilizers needed as a base dressing, to be forked in lightly 7–10 days before planting. Cultivate the soil some weeks before planting by digging in organic matter such as well-rotted manure, mushroom or garden compost, or peat, and water well. Depending on the crop and its vigour, additional feeding during growth may be required, as a top dressing of solid fertilizer or liquid feed.

Container-grown glasshouse plants can be raised in composts made up of a variety of different media as long as they provide the plant with anchorage and stability, and its roots with air, water and nutrients. A balance between small air spaces in the compost, which hold water, and large air spaces, which carry oxygen to the roots, is essential. Most common glasshouse plants require a compost that is moisture-retentive and free-draining to prevent saturation. In waterlogged composts, where the pores are saturated, respiration cannot take place and the roots will eventually die.

For the new glasshouse gardener, with limited space, it is simplest to buy proprietary, ready-made composts which are ideal for the majority of glasshouse plants. It is helpful to know what makes up these proprietary brands and the accompanying chart of compost ingredients should be a useful reference now and also in the future if you decide to start mixing your own composts.

Composts are divided into two main groups – soil-based, with loam as the main ingredient, and soilless, with peat usually the main ingredient.

Soil-based composts

Soil-based composts are best made up of a mixture of sterilized loam (from stacked turfs) and peat and grit to provide an open structure. The loam holds on to nutrients providing more consistent nutrient levels than most soilless composts, and as minor nutrients are present in sufficient quantities in loam, they will not need to be added. They are also heavier and give more stability to large or top-heavy plants, such as standard fuchsias.

Standard soil-based composts may be bought made up to the John Innes Institute formulae for seed and potting composts. These contain a base fertilizer and in the potting compost the fertilizer comes in different strengths, sold as John Innes Potting Composts Nos. 1, 2 and 3, No. 3 having three times as much fertilizer as No. 1. After a few weeks plants will benefit from additional feeding during their growing season (see page 52).

COMPOST FORMULATIONS

Ingredients	Purpose
Soil-based	
Seed-sowing compost	
2 parts (by bulk) sterilized loam	Provides 'body', trace elements and weight. Helps reduce nitrogen leaching.
1 part (by bulk) peat	Assists aeration and moisture retention.
1 part (by bulk) sharp sand	Provides weight and drainage.
Fertilizers added per m³ of compost:	
1.2kg superphosphate	Provides phosphate, calcium and sulphur.
0.58kg ground limestone or chalk	Neutralizes acidity of peat and loam.
Potting compost	
7 parts (by bulk) loam	As seed compost.
3 parts (by bulk) peat	As seed compost.
2 parts (by bulk) sharp sand	As seed compost.
Fertilizers added per m³ of compost:	
John Innes No.1:	Suitable for pricking out or first potting.
2.92kg base fertilizer (see below)	
0.58kg ground limestone or chalk	
John Innes No.2:	Suitable as general potting mix.
Add twice as much John Innes base fertilizer.	
John Innes No.3:	Suitable for plants with high feed
Add three times as much John Innes base fertilizer.	requirements such as chrysanthemums.
The base fertilizer is made up by weight:	
2 parts hoof and horn	Slow-release source of nitrogen.
2 parts superphosphate	Provides phosphate, calcium and sulphur.
1 part sulphate of potash	Provides potassium.
Soilless	
Cutting mix	
1 part (by bulk) peat or coir fibre	Provides aeration and drainage and assists moisture retention.
1 part (by bulk) sharp sand	Provides drainage and stability.
No fertilizer required.	
Seed-sowing compost	
3 parts (by bulk) peat	As above.
1 part (by bulk) sharp sand	As above.
Fertilizer per m³ of compost:	
0.75kg superphosphate	As above.
0.4kg potassium nitrate	Provides potassium and nitrogen.
3kg ground limestone or chalk	Neutralizes acidity.
Potting compost	
3 parts (by bulk) peat	As above
1 part (by bulk) sharp sand	As above
Fertilizer per m³ of compost:	
4–4.8kg ground limestone or chalk and a base fertilizer containing a balanced supply of major and minor nutrients.	
Peat-based with low loam	
Potting compost	
5 parts (by bulk) peat	As above.
1 part (by bulk) sharp sand	As above.
1 part (by bulk) loam	As above.
Fertilizer: as above	

NUTRIENT CHART

Chemical	Use	Deficiency	Excess
Nitrogen (N)	Required at all times by plants. Component of green chlorophyll in plants.	Stunted growth. Foliage pale green, yellow or reddish-yellow. Lack of vigour.	Soft fleshy growth. Failure to flower and fruit in some cases.
Phosphorus (P)	Important for germination, root production and seed/fruit ripening. Required in smaller amounts than nitrogen.	Lower leaves small, dark green with purplish undersides. Plants stunted with restricted shoot and root growth. Flowering reduced.	Only a problem with sensitive plants such as proteas. Shows up as yellowing between leaf veins.
Potassium (K) (potash)	Encourages flowering and helps to produce strong, healthy, disease-resistant growth by thickening cell walls.	Decreases in availability in very acid or alkaline composts. Marginal scorching on foliage. Die-back of shoots in severe cases.	Prevents uptake of magnesium. Potassium induces magnesium deficiency.
Calcium (Ca)	Makes up part of cell wall, therefore required at growing tips.	Distorted and curled young foliage. Death of leaf margins and tips. Death of shoot tips. Soil acid (low pH).	Makes soil alkaline (high pH). Prevents uptake of iron. Makes phosphates insoluble.
Magnesium (Mg)	Forms part of chlorophyll essential for photosynthesis.	Caused by high potassium levels. Yellowing between veins in older leaves. Leaf margins curl upwards.	Prevents uptake of potassium and calcium.
Sulphur (S)	Important in the plant's biochemistry in synthesis of proteins and enzymes.	Young foliage pale, leaves sometimes rolled downward or with reddish tints.	Rarely a problem.
Iron (Fe)	Essential in the synthesis of chlorophyll.	Yellowing between veins in young foliage.	Induces manganese deficiency.
Molybdenum (Mo)	Important in metabolism of nitrogen.	Yellowing of older leaves. Marginal wilting. Distortion of leaves and stems.	Leaves turn golden-yellow, sometimes with blue tinge.
Boron (B)	Assists movement of materials within the plants.	Death of stem and root tips. Young leaves blacken and shrivel.	Margins of old leaves yellow followed by scorching.
Copper (Cu)	Plays a part in photosynthesis.	Scorching of leaf tips extended to margins.	Induces iron deficiency and stunting of roots and shoots.
Manganese (Mn)	Involved in many aspects of plant metabolism.	Yellowing between leaf veins and yellow, water-soaked spots.	Induces iron deficiency. Produces cupping and yellowing of leaf margins.
Zinc (Zn)	Essential for cell enlargement.	Reduced leaf size and internode length producing a stunted plant.	As for iron deficiency.

The chart opposite shows how the different types of compost are made up and what the different ingredients provide. The chart above shows the nutrients that are required for healthy plant growth.

Soilless composts

Peat has been the primary potting compost ingredient for the last 20 years because of the consistency and reliability of supplies. Peat-based composts are lightweight and give a good balance of air and water. Some contain sand or grit to aid drainage and also to increase their weight, giving more stability to potted plants. As peat contains few nutrients naturally, slow-release fertilizers with minor nutrients or regular liquid feeding (see page 52) are essential.

Medium-grade sphagnum moss is the preferred

type of peat because of its excellent air- and water-holding capacity. Composts containing sedge peat have a finer texture, are more acidic, and also require careful watering. Some proprietary composts, however, contain ingredients such as vermiculite, perlite, perlag or rockwool, which help to improve aeration and water retention.

Recent environmental concerns over the harvesting of peat has prompted the horticultural industry to look for alternatives. The most promising for pot plant growing appears to be coir – a waste product of the coconut fibre industry. It is available as a ready-made potting compost from most garden centres, but is expensive.

Multi-purpose composts

These are intended for both seed sowing and potting, and are either soil- or peat-based. They contain a lower level of nutrients than potting composts, to prevent sensitive seedlings from scorching, which means that supplementary liquid feeding is required when they are used for potting. I have not included multi-purpose composts in the accompanying chart as they are made up to a variety of specifications.

Nutrients

Nutrients are vital for healthy plants. Nitrogen (N), phosphorus (P) and potassium (K) are required in large quantities; magnesium, calcium and sulphur in medium quantities; and the minor nutrients (trace elements) – iron, boron, manganese, copper, zinc and molybdenum – in small quantities.

The acidity or alkalinity of a compost is vital as it affects how efficiently plants take in nutrients. It is measured on a pH scale of 1–14, numbers below 7 being acid and those above alkaline. The ideal pH for the healthy growth of most plants is pH 6.5, which is slightly acid. However, certain ericaceous plants, such as heathers, like an acid compost with a pH below 6. It is possible to neutralize the acidity of a compost by adding lime but alkalinity cannot be changed easily. Use a soil testing kit to discover the pH of your compost.

Feeding

Regular feeding throughout the spring and summer is necessary for flowering plants, such as Salpiglossis sinuata *and zonal pelargonium cultivars, to maintain their vigour.*

Artificial feeding is not as important in the garden where plants have a larger root run and a balance of nutrients is available naturally from the decomposition of fallen leaves and other organic matter. In the controlled environment of the glasshouse, however, where plants are grown in pots and their root systems are restricted, nutrients in the compost are soon depleted, and fertilizers need to be added to sustain healthy growth. This is usually provided by liquid feeding (see below). The nutrients required by plants are described on page 51.

Types of fertilizer

Fertilizers are available in organic or inorganic form; organic fertilizers are either plant (such as seaweed) or animal (such as hoof and horn) in origin, while inorganic fertilizers are manufactured from minerals. Most organic fertilizers are broken down slowly by bacteria, making the nutrients available to plants over a period of time – in the case of hoof and horn for up to five months. Inorganic fertilizers are fast-acting as their nutrients are released quickly. They also tend to be cheaper as they contain by weight a higher percentage of nutrients. Always follow the manufacturer's instructions closely when using fertilizers. Scorching of the leaves will result if fertilizers are used at too high a concentration.

Fertilizers are grouped according to the way they supply their nutrients. Straight fertilizers supply only one major nutrient – for example, ammonium nitrate fertilizer provides nitrogen. Compound or general fertilizers supply two or more nutrients – potassium nitrate, for example, giving potassium and nitrogen. When buying compound fertilizers check what ratio of nitrogen, phosphorus and potassium (N, P and K) they contain. At the start of the growing season when vigorous growth is required, a fertilizer with high nitrogen should be selected – this is indicated by an N:P:K ratio of 3:1:1. Later in the season, when a balanced growth is needed, use an N:P:K ratio of 1:1:1. An N:P:K ratio of 1:1:2 will help harden up growth for the winter and promote flowering. Slow-release fertilizers can be straight or compound and release their nutrients gradually to plants. Resin-coated, slow-release fertilizers are manufactured in different formulations which enable them to release their nutrients over a predetermined period of 3, 6, or 12 months.

Liquid feeds

Liquid feeding is the usual method of supplying additional nutrients to container-grown plants. Unless the compost contains slow-release fertilizers, supplementary liquid feeding will be necessary after only a few weeks to top up nutrient deficiencies. Liquid feeds may be bought in concentrated form containing nitrogen, phosphate and potassium (potash) in different ratios and may include minor nutrients (trace elements). They are diluted with water according to the manufacturer's instructions and then watered into the pot so that the nutrients can be taken up by the roots. Container-grown plants require feeding most often in summer – once or twice a week – when growth is rapid and frequent watering causes nutrients to leach. In winter it can be cut down to as little as once or twice a month, depending on the plant and outside weather conditions. Too much liquid feeding will result in the build-up of fertilizer residues in the compost, causing an excess of salt which will scorch plant roots, and the plant will exhibit marginal leaf burn. This is remedied by flushing the containers through with clean water.

If only a few plants need feeding, the liquid feed can be made up in a watering can, following the manufacturer's instructions, and watered in using a fine circular rose. If many plants need feeding, you could use a proportional diluter fixed to the garden hose. This injects feed at the required concentration into the water flowing through the hose. It is essential, however, to fit a non-return valve to the tap to prevent contaminated water siphoning back into the mains water system.

Foliar feeds

Some liquid feeds are absorbed through the leaves as well as the roots. These are called foliar feeds, and are particularly useful for cuttings which have inadequate root systems. The advantage of foliar feeding is that the nutrients are absorbed very quickly. It is, however, expensive as only half of the nutrients in the feed are absorbed by the leaves. Foliar feeds should be mixed according to the manufacturers instructions and applied with a watering can and fine rose, or a fine mist hand sprayer to ensure a thorough coverage. Avoid foliar feeding in bright sunshine as this can scorch the foliage.

COMPONENTS OF COMMON FERTILIZERS

FERTILIZER	Nutrients Provided			Other nutrients	Notes
	N	P	K		
Ammonium nitrate	34%	–	–		I – quick acting. Used in compost base and liquid feeds.
Potassium nitrate	13.8%	–	39%		I – quick acting. Used in compost base.
Nitrochalk	26%	–	–	Carbonate of lime in varying concentrations.	I – quick acting.
Urea	45%	–	–		O – slow-release.
Hoof and horn	13%	–	–		O – slow-release.
Dried blood	10–13%	–	–		O – quick-acting.
Fish meal	8–10%	2–4%	1.5–2.5%		O – available in powder or concentrated liquid form.
Superphosphate	–	8%	–	Sulphur 11%, Calcium 21%	I – used as base dressing in borders and compost.
Triple superphosphate	–	21%	–		I – base dressing.
Mono ammonium phosphate	11.8%	26%	–		I – contained in slow-release fertilizers.
Bonemeal	1–5%	6.5–14%	–		O – apply to borders low in phosphates.
Sulphate of potash	–	–	45%		I – apply as quick-acting source of potash.
Seaweed	0.4–0.8%	0.1–0.2%	1–2%		O – available as a powder or in liquid form.
Epsom salts (Magnesium sulphate)	–	–	–	9% magnesium	I – corrects magnesium deficiency.
Magnesium limestone	–	–	–	Magnesium and calcium carbonate	I – supplies lime to help reduce acidity.
Ground limestone	–	–	–	Calcium carbonate	I – as for Magnesium limestone.
Fritted trace elements	–	–	–	Balanced minor nutrients	I – slow-release. Only one application required.
Chelated trace elements	–	–	–	As above	I – water soluble form. Immediately available to plants. Used as a foliar or compost application.
Chelated iron	–	–	–	Iron	I – soluble form of iron. Apply as foliar or soil drench.

I=Inorganic   O=Organic

COMPOUND FERTILIZERS

Compound fertilizers in both slow-release and liquid form are available in a variety of ratios to suit particular crops.

Fertilizer	N:P:K: Ratio	Uses
John Innes Base	1:1.5:2	General balanced base fertilizer as used in John Innes composts.
Slow-release	Available in a wide range.	Suitable for supplying nutrients over a long period of time.
	Similar to liquid below.	Inorganic slow-release fertilizers are ideal for peat-based composts.
Liquid feeds	2:1:1	Spring and summer feed for chrysanthemums.
		All stages for bedding plants.
		Spring/summer feed for pot plants and foliage plants.
	3:0:1	Promote rapid spring growth in shrubs and bedding plants.
	2:1:4	Main feed for cucumbers.
		Autumn/winter feed for chrysanthemums and pot plants.
		Spring/summer feed for tomatoes.
	1:1:1	Late summer boost for tomatoes.
		Main summer feed for carnations (Dianthus).
		Spring/autumn feed for pot plants.
	1:1:2	Promote flowering in pot plants.
		Main feed for peppers and aubergines.

Watering

The health of all plants is dependent on the correct amount of moisture in a compost. I am frequently asked by people how often they should water their glasshouse plants but there is no set answer as each plant has its own individual requirements. Many bedding plants grown under glass originate from warmer, more humid climates where there is plenty of moisture and so their leaves are large and lose a lot of water. Such plants will need much more watering than, for example, many cacti with their succulent stems which retain moisture.

All plants will dry out more quickly in warm, dry and draughty conditions which increase water loss from the leaves. Plants that are actively growing require extra water to expand their cells and a pot-bound plant which has less space in the pot to hold moisture will dry out quickly, sometimes needing watering twice a day. During the short days of winter, when the glasshouse is cooler and humid, little growth takes place and plants can stay moist for many weeks.

The best method of finding out if a plant requires water is to feel the compost in the pot with your fingers to see if it is moist or dry. Soilless composts should always feel slightly moist because, if allowed to dry out too much, they will crack away from the pot and make re-wetting difficult. Soil-based composts should be allowed to become almost dry at the surface between waterings as the small particles of soil can hold a large reservoir of water. Another method of testing whether a plant in a clay pot needs watering is to tap the pot with a wooden stick. A wet pot will produce a duller tone than a dry one. If you have a small number of pots filled with soilless composts, lift the pots to assess the weight. A pot containing moist compost weighs more than one with dry compost.

Meters are available for testing soil moisture but are useful only for the absolute beginner who has no experience of watering plants. They are intended only as guides for watering, giving the average water requirement for the average plant. During the summer it is important to check glasshouse plants for watering at least twice a day.

Plants are best watered in the morning, although on hot days in summer vigorous plants may need a second watering, which can take place from midday to late afternoon, but no later, to allow excess moisture to evaporate before nightfall. Plants prefer water that has been allowed to stand to reach the ambient glasshouse temperature. By keeping a tank of water in the glasshouse (see page 23), a supply of water of the correct temperature will always be available. Very cold water should not be used as this can be a shock to plants, and splashes will cause blemishes on the leaves of plants such as african violets (*Saintpaulia ionantha*).

Rainwater can be collected from the house and glasshouse roofs (see page 23), and, unless you live in an area of high pollution, it should be free of mineral and chemical contaminates. Tap water is suitable for most plants, although ericaceous plants, azaleas and heathers for example, will suffer – their foliage will yellow and they will eventually die – if watered with hard water which contains a high proportion of dissolved calcium. Established plants may be watered with an open hose or watering can as long as the pressure is low, which will prevent the compost from being blasted. Newly potted plants and seedlings must be watered with a watering can and fine rose to avoid disturbing the loose surface compost and exposing the young roots to desiccation (see page 40).

When watering fill the gap between the soil and the top of the pot as the water will permeate through all the compost in the pot. If plants are given small doses of water, only the top half of the compost will get wet and the bottom of the pot will remain dry, hindering root development.

The glasshouse border may be watered by hand with a watering can and oval rose or with a rose attached to a hand-held hose. The most efficient method of watering large borders is to use seep hoses or drip tubes, which are attached to a pressurized water supply, to give an even flow of water to the roots of each plant (see page 35).

Achimenes grandiflora

The popular name for this plant is the hot water plant, so called because cold water splashed on to the foliage will cause unsightly discoloration. However, if watering is carried out carefully, cold water can be used as long as it does not touch the foliage. In winter, plants must be kept dry so that they die back to maggot-like rhizomes which are repotted and started into growth in late winter. Attractive, rose-pink flowers are produced in profusion in summer.

Pests and diseases

The warm, protected environment of the glasshouse not only encourages plants to grow well but also allows a wide range of pests and diseases to flourish, which, if not checked, will hamper the healthy growth of your plants.

Pests

Pests are animals that cause damage to plants, whether spider mites smaller than a pin-head feeding on the sap of a plant, or deer chewing the bark of trees. Glasshouse pests can generally be divided into two categories – those that chew and eat parts of a plant, such as slugs, and those that suck sap, such as mealy bugs, feeding off plants in much the same way that mosquitoes feed off us!

The damage caused by chewing pests is noticed easily. When holes appear in the leaves, the culprit can usually be found by picking up the plant and shaking it to see if any caterpillars fall off, or examining under the pot for slugs.

Sucking pests are not noticed so easily as they are mostly tiny and feed on the undersides of leaves and other out-of-the-way places. Identification of the pest must then be made from the symptoms. A frequent tell-tale sign of their presence is a sugary substance on the foliage. This is known as honey dew and is excreted by many insects. If left, the honey dew will be colonized by fungi, forming a black layer similar to soot – hence its common name of 'sooty mould'. Other sucking pests, such as aphids, feed on young buds and leaves and the first sign of their presence is distorted and puckered foliage.

Diseases

Diseases are caused by microscopic organisms such as fungi, bacteria and viruses which may severely affect the growth of a plant.

Fungi are mostly recognized by their fruiting bodies, such as the white leaf covering of powdery mildew, the fluffy grey-white growths of mould and the rusty red spots on foliage and stems caused by rust fungi. Other fungi present in the soil will attack roots and stems and cause damping off.

Yellow sticky traps are placed above infected plants to attract and catch flying insects. They are also very useful for monitoring the pest population in the glasshouse.

Bacterial damage can result in lesions, commonly called cankers, or soft rots but, as a rule, bacterial disorders are difficult to distinguish and require the trained eye of an expert.

Viruses, such as tobacco mosaic virus and tomato mosaic virus, may be spread from plant to plant by sap-sucking insects such as aphids and sometimes by taking cuttings from infected plants and transmitting their sap, on the knife, to healthy plants. Viruses usually affect the vigour of a plant, and may show up as distorted or blemished foliage – blotches, concentric ring-spots, spots, yellow mosaic or mottled areas. They can also reduce the yields of fruit and vegetable crops drastically. There is no cure for viral diseases. Infected plants should be removed and destroyed to prevent any disease from spreading.

Physiological disorders

Any plant malady not caused by a pest or disease is termed a physiological disorder, and is usually cultural in origin. Yellowing of the foliage and eventual leaf fall and death can result from over-watering, while extreme dry or draughty conditions may cause marginal leaf scorch. Deficiencies of certain nutrients in the compost, such as iron or manganese, may result in yellowing foliage (see the nutrient chart on page 51).

Cultural control

Plants, like ourselves, are less susceptible to disease if they are in a healthy state, and those gardeners who practise good husbandry should have fewer problems. However, even the most carefully grown plant is not immune from attack. When introducing new plants to the glasshouse, it is important to check them over closely as most pests are introduced on new plants. Weeds in and around the glasshouse should be controlled as they too are often hosts to pests and diseases, such as whitefly and western flower thrip. It is a good idea to have an isolation area in your glasshouse where new plants can be separated for a few weeks to see if any problems occur.

Plants should be checked regularly, at least twice a week, for the development of any pest or disease – a magnifying glass will make some of the smaller pests easier to track down. Yellow sticky traps which are plastic cards covered with a sticky, clear grease help to monitor pest populations and also control some of them, attracting and catching many flying insects. They are available in various sizes and should be hung up approximately 15cm (6in) above the plants. They will need to be replaced regularly, before they become plastered with insects.

Where small numbers of pests are spotted, it is often much easier to squash and wipe them off with a damp cloth or remove the infected leaf. Only when this is impractical should you resort to chemical or biological controls.

Chemical control

All chemicals used to control pests and diseases are generally known as pesticides. More specifically, insecticides control insects and fungicides control fungal disorders.

In recent years there has been a greater awareness of the hazards involved in spraying certain pesticides and this has resulted in the restricted use of some and a total removal from sale of others. In addition, continuous use of the same pesticides to control particular pests and diseases has led to them becoming resistant to the pesticide and therefore difficult to control. A new generation of apparently safer chemicals is now coming on to the market.

Chemicals are split into contact and systemic pesticides. A contact pesticide kills on contact with the pest, either directly from the spray or from residues persisting on the plant. A systemic pesticide is translocated through the plant tissues and absorbed by feeding pests or diseases. Systemic pesticides are generally more persistent.

It is very important when using chemicals to follow the manufacturers' instructions on the label to ensure the safety of the environment, yourself and your plants.

Biological control

The aim of biological control is to manipulate the natural enemies of a pest in order to reduce their numbers and keep them at an acceptable level. Biological controls are divided into two categories – predators which attack and eat the pest, and parasites which inject their eggs into the pest resulting in the pest's death. Most of these controls are effective only where daytime temperatures exceed 18°C (65°F). They are available by mail order and from good garden centres.

Integrated pest management is where a balance of biological controls and non-persistent chemicals is used to control a wide range of pests in an environmentally-friendly way. As many pests have developed resistance to frequently used pesticides, integrated pest management is gaining popularity. If pest numbers are high, one particularly effective method is first to apply horticultural soap, which works by drowning the pest, or another non-persistent chemical to the affected plants. Then introduce the biological control, as directed by the supplier who should also provide you with information on the time lapse required between applying the chemical and the biological controls. They should never be applied at the same time as the chemical control may harm the beneficial predator or parasite.

Depending upon the pest, a number of introductions of the control may be necessary. For example, *Phytoseiulus persimilis* is such a successful predator that it kills off all its prey of red spider mites leaving itself with no food and so starves to death. If the pest re-emerges, the predator will need to be reintroduced.

Plants exhibiting disorders can be checked off against the accompanying chart which will suggest the likely pest or disease and give the appropriate treatment.

PESTS AND DISEASES

Pest	Symptoms	Treatment
Root-eating/Soil-inhabiting		
Root aphids Live on young roots near soil surface and on edge of pots. Covered with white wool or meal.	Plant droops. Shoots die back.	Suitable insecticidal contact drench to compost. Wash pest and compost off roots and repot in sterilized compost, or take cuttings and dispose of plant.
Root mealy bugs Similar to root aphids, covered in wax.	As for root aphids.	As for root aphids.
Sciarid flies and larvae Tiny grey-black flies. Larvae approx. 3mm (1/8in) long thrive in moist compost where they appear as small white maggots with black heads.	Root damage. Slowed growth. Death of seedlings and soft cuttings.	Water less frequently. Remove dead leaves from soil surface. † Parasitic nematode (microscopic round worm) as a soil drench up to 4 times during growing season *or* suitable insecticidal contact drench.
Slugs and snails	Chewed foliage/stems/flowers. Silvery trails.	Slug bait and contact sprays.
Vine weevils Curved, creamy white, plump larvae with brown heads, over 1cm (1/2in) long, found feeding among roots. Beetle-like adults found on foliage.	Wilting. Chewed roots. Leaf margins eaten by adults.	Squash the adults which are seen only at night. † Parasitic nematode (microscopic round worm), applied as above.
Foliage-eating		
Aphids Green- or blackfly – may also be yellow or pink.	Honeydew and sooty mould. Stunted, distorted growth.	Remove small infestations with moist cotton wool. Horticultural soap. † *Chrysoperla carnea* (lacewing); *Aphidoletes aphidimyza*; *Aphidius matricariae*, or suitable contact insecticide.
Caterpillars	Uneven cuts on leaves. Excreta on foliage. Leaves tightly webbed together with silk.	Destroy caterpillars by hand. † Spray with *Bacillus thuringiensis or* suitable contact insecticide.
Glasshouse leafhoppers Approx. 3mm (1/8in) long with slender, tapering body. Found on underside of leaves. Jump and fly from leaf to leaf when disturbed.	Coarse white mottling on upper surface of leaves. Underside of leaves covered with moulted skins.	Remove leaves covered in eggs, although difficult to see. Suitable contact insecticide.
Leaf miners Larvae of fly, moth and beetle species. Visible in leaf mines as small grubs approx. 3mm (1/8in) long.	Irregular blotches on leaves. Wiggly brown or white lines on foliage.	Remove and destroy mined leaves. † *Dacnusa sibirica*; *Diglyphus isaea or* suitable systemic insecticide.
Mealy bugs Small insects covered in white waxy secretion found on growing points and leaf joints.	Similar to aphid infestation (see above).	Horticultural soap. † *Cryptolaemus montrouzieri* (black ladybird) if temperatures over 21°C (70°F) *or* suitable contact or systemic insecticide.
Scale insects Tiny whitish, yellowish, or brown scale-like insects on stems/leaves.	Similar to aphid infestation (see above). Honeydew, yellowing and defoliation.	Remove adult scales with moist cotton wool. Adult scales resistant to most chemicals. Kill young scales with horticultural soap. Suitable systemic insecticide.
Two-spotted or red spider mites Yellowish-green with two distinct darker spots on the front of the body during the summer. Turn orange-red prior to hibernation.	Fine yellow speckles on foliage. Shrivelled and dead leaves. Silken threads over plant in severe cases.	Keep humidity high. Dampen undersides of foliage. † *Phytoseiulus persimilis or* suitable systemic insecticide.

Pest	Symptoms	Treatment
Western flower thrips Adults are approx. 1mm (1/16in) long and grey/yellow-brown in colour. Can seriously affect flowering pot plants such as streptocarpus, and crops such as cucumbers.	Silvering and mottling of foliage and flowers. Stunted growth in severe cases. Distortion of fruit.	Remove and destroy faded flowers containing thrips. Resistant to most chemicals. † *Amblyseius cucumeris*; *Amblyseius barkeri*; anthocorid bugs when above 20°C (68°F).
Whiteflies Egg-laying adults are tiny, white, moth-like insects, found on youngest foliage. Immature, scale-like stages found on older foliage. Serious pest for most glasshouse plants.	Honeydew and sooty mould. Yellowing and defoliation in severe cases.	Resistant to most insecticides. Horticultural soap. † *Encarsia formosa* (parasitic wasp) once daytime temperatures are over 15°C (60°F).

Disease	Symptoms	Treatment
Black leg Soil-borne fungi. Frequent problem with pelargoniums.	Blackening on the stem of a cutting, causing it to shrivel and die.	Use pots free of fungal spores (see under Damping off). Use only sterilized compost. Use clean water. Suitable fungicide.
Damping off Caused by soil- and water-borne fungi.	Young seedlings collapse and die at soil level.	Ensure good hygiene. Use sterilized compost for seed sowing. Wash all containers before use in a proprietary disinfectant to kill off any fungal spores, and rinse well afterwards. Water in seed with a suitable fungicide. Do not sow seed too thickly and prick out when seed leaves are fully expanded.
Downy mildew Caused by a variety of fungal parasites. Favours humid conditions.	Yellowish patches on leaves. Whitish mould on underside.	Remove infected foliage. Improve air circulation around plant. Avoid splashing leaves with water. Suitable fungicide.
Grey mould (*Botrytis*) Thrives in damp conditions.	Fluffy grey fungal growth. Water-soaked foliage. Pale spotting on flowers.	Remove infected plant material and debris. Improve air circulation around plant. Avoid splashing foliage in humid conditions. Suitable fungicide.
Oedema Caused by the plant taking up more water from its roots than it can lose through its leaves by transpiration.	Warty growths on the stem and underside of leaves.	Reduce watering. Increase spacing. Improve ventilation. Do *not* remove leaves as this will slow down water loss.
Powdery mildew Spread by spores in leaf debris and in the air.	Powdery white coating on leaves and stems. Yellowing and defoliation.	Remove infected leaves and stems. Keep roots more moist. Improve air circulation around plant. Suitable fungicide.
Rust Variable disease which can affect many different plants.	Pale yellow spots on leaves. Orange or brown spots on the underside of leaves. Stunted and distorted growth.	Remove infected leaves. Improve air circulation around plant. Suitable fungicide.
Sooty mould Grows on honeydew excreted by sap-sucking insects such as aphids, whitefly, scale insects and mealy bugs.	Black sooty deposits on leaves. Reduction in plant vigour in severe cases.	Control the insect pest, and then remove mould with a moistened sponge.
Tobacco mosaic virus Affects a wide range of plants in many plant families. Spread by pests such as aphids.	Leaf mottling and distortion. Weak, stunted growth.	Destroy infected plants. Control virus-spreading pests.
Tomato mosaic virus	As for tobacco mosaic virus.	As for tobaco mosaic virus.

†=Biological Control

THE PRODUCTIVE GLASSHOUSE

The greatest concern for anyone new to glasshouse gardening is knowing what to grow and how best to plan and use the available space. In the previous chapter various glasshouse tasks – from propagating through to feeding and watering – have been described, and in this chapter advice is given on how to turn the glasshouse into a hive of activity supporting the flower, fruit and vegetable garden.

Container-grown fruit and vegetables can be raised all year round in the cool glasshouse. Tomatoes and peppers planted in growing bags or long-life paper pots allow a more versatile use of the glasshouse space, although regular watering and feeding are vital to ensure a continued supply of produce over summer.

THE PRODUCTIVE GLASSHOUSE

Planning and organization

It is very easy to be overwhelmed by the seductive descriptions and pictures of plants in seed catalogues and order much more seed than you want or can cope with. For the first-time grower it is best to gain experience by raising predictable plants, such as bedding plants and vegetables, before attempting to grow exotic plants, such as orchids, which are very specific in their growing requirements.

Most gardeners enjoy the challenge of growing and cultivating plants as much as the satisfaction of the finished product, whether a perfectly grown pelargonium, a good crop of tasty tomatoes or a garden full of home-raised bedding plants. Having a fully productive glasshouse is no easy matter as, more often than not, the glasshouse is full of young plants in the spring, all jostling for space, but more or less empty once the bedding plants have been planted out in late spring to early summer. All that remains is probably a few tomato plants!

When organizing your glasshouse for production,

This well-organized glasshouse is fitted with a glazed division to create two temperature regimes – one warmer for propagation and one cooler for growing on, with pot plants displayed on the staging and tomatoes planted in the border.

it is essential to know in advance when your plants will start to take up space and exactly how much they will need. Once you have run a glasshouse for a few seasons it is possible to know from experience how to organize your space. For those new to glasshouse gardening, however, it pays to work it out on paper first to avoid errors and disappointment. First of all, decide which plants you wish to grow and how many of each you require. Then, with the help of this book and seed catalogues, work out when seed should be sown and cuttings taken; how long the rooting/germination period is; when the plants should be potted and potted on; and when they are ready to leave the glasshouse for the garden.

It is then possible to see how different crops will be competing with each other for space. You can easily work out how much each crop will need by multiplying the final space taken up by one plant by the number of plants required. It is not unusual to find that you need a glasshouse three times the size to cope with your aspirations. If this is the case, priorities have to be worked out – perhaps grow a smaller number of each plant type, or grow some plants earlier in the season and harden them off sooner in a cold frame to make space in the glasshouse for plants from a later sowing.

Most glasshouse growing can be tackled with a frame, except where extra height is needed. In fact, an ideal propagation unit is made up of a glasshouse, a heated propagator and cold frames covering an area roughly equivalent to that of the glasshouse. But the best tools any gardener can have are enthusiasm, observation and a little ingenuity. Each year many fine plants are grown under the most basic conditions but the gardener manages to supply all the plants' requirements. For example, if you have only a frost-free glasshouse, you can raise your plants in home-made propagators covered with polythene in the warm environment of a window sill. Once the weather gets warmer, the plants can be grown on in the glasshouse, and hardened off in a home-made frame of concrete blocks supporting an old glazed window frame.

Raising garden plants

The glasshouse can be used to raise a whole range of hardy and half-hardy plants, tender perennials and bedding plants for the garden.

Hardy plants

Hardy plants can be propagated very easily in the glasshouse by taking cuttings or sowing seed. These plants can then be used to great effect in the garden.

Cuttings

These should be inserted in a rooting medium in a heated propagation environment or cold frame. Softwood cuttings are taken from plants in rapid growth in spring and early summer and, because of their sappy nature, root best in a heated propagator or warm bench and polythene tent. It is vital that these cuttings are not allowed to dry out at any time as they wilt very easily.

Cuttings inserted directly into a cold frame will need a minimal amount of maintenance as they dry out more slowly in the closed humid atmosphere of the frame than they would in a sunny glasshouse. The frame should be insulated, with brick or wooden sides and in a well-lit position but shaded from direct sunlight. The site should be well drained and the soil forked over to assist drainage. Add a layer of equal parts peat and sharp sand, approximately 15cm (6in) deep, as a rooting medium.

Herbaceous plants and shrubs Softwood and semi-ripe cuttings 5–10cm (2–4in) long are prepared in early to mid-summer. They should be inserted either in pots or trays in a heated propagation environment in an unheated glasshouse (see page 39), or in rows directly into a cold frame, with their foliage just touching. When the frame is full, water in the cuttings and put the frame lights in place. The frame will need to be covered with a shading fabric to stop it from overheating and the plants from 'cooking'. Check the cuttings regularly, removing any diseased or dead leaves that would encourage the spread of grey mould (*Botrytis*). Once

rooting has taken place (in two to four weeks in the glasshouse, five to six weeks in the cold frame), the cuttings must be gradually hardened off, that is, acclimatized to exposed conditions. If you are using a propagator, follow the advice on page 45. If you are using a cold frame, increase the ventilation and remove the shade cloth. By late summer you can leave off the frame lights altogether. Once hardened off, the rooted cuttings can be potted up into 9cm (3½in) pots and placed in the cold frame or unheated glasshouse, to establish before winter.

Evergreen shrubs From late summer to early autumn, semi-ripe heel cuttings can be taken and inserted either in a heated propagation environment in an unheated glasshouse, or directly into a cold frame which must be checked regularly and shaded from bright sun. During frosty periods the cuttings must be insulated from the cold by covering the lights with an insulating material such as an old, thick carpet. Keep the frame lights closed over the cuttings during cold weather until early spring by which time rooting should have taken place. The cuttings can then be hardened off and should be ready for potting up in mid-spring.

Seed

The seed of hardy plants should be sown in pots and trays on the surface of compost and covered with coarse grit. The pots should then be placed on a level, well-drained medium, such as medium-sized grit, in a cold frame or unheated glasshouse. Most seed is sown in early spring but if you are using seed collected from your garden plants, it may be later; for example, hardy cyclamen and primulas should be sown in late summer.

Some plants contain germination inhibitors in their seed coat as a natural survival mechanism to spread germination out over a period of time and thus ensure the survival of some of the progeny. Seed from such plants need a period of damp cold to break down chemicals in the seed coat, allowing germination to take place in spring. This is known as

HARDY PLANTS FROM SOFTWOOD AND SEMI-RIPE CUTTINGS

Cytisus scoparius (common broom)
Erica carnea cultivars
Philadelphus coronarius
Phlox paniculata
Potentilla fruticosa
Senecio 'Sunshine'

HARDY PLANTS FROM SEMI-RIPE HEEL CUTTINGS

Cotoneaster congestus
Escallonia 'Edinensis'
Garrya elliptica
Hebe albicans
Lavandula angustifolia 'Munstead'
Skimmia japonica

HARDY PLANTS FROM SEED

Acer platanoides: stratify for 4 months at 5°C (41°F)
Berberis species: stratify for 15–40 days at 0–5°C (32–41°F)
Clematis species: stratify for 3 months at 5°C (41°F)
Cupressus species: stratify for 2 months at 5°C (41°F)
Magnolia species: stratify for 6 months at 5°C (41°F)
Robinia pseudoacacia: scarify seed before sowing

stratification. The seed of *Sorbus* and many *Cotoneaster* species, for example, can be mixed with moist vermiculite and placed in a plastic bag in the refrigerator for three to six months before sowing in spring. However, seed will germinate on its own accord in a pot left in an unheated glasshouse or cold frame, although it may sometimes take a few years for them all to germinate.

Berries are often surrounded by a pulp which contains germination inhibitors. If this is the case, separate the seed from its pulp and rinse in water before drying off on a sheet of blotting paper. Seed such as *Robinia* or *Acacia* have hard, impermeable coats. Either soak them in hot water which is allowed to cool before being drained off, or abrade part of the coat with sandpaper – this process is known as scarification – which will allow moisture to swell the seed after it has been sown.

The seed of hardy plants can be germinated in a cold frame protected from direct sunlight to avoid fluctuations in temperature, or in an unheated glasshouse. As soon as the seed has germinated, move the seedlings out of the humid atmosphere to the open bench or ventilated frame.

Tender perennials and half-hardy plants

There are many tender and half-hardy plants worth raising each year, all of which can be propagated from cuttings taken in late summer and over-wintered in a frost-free frame or glasshouse. Once they start to grow in spring they should be potted up into 9cm (3½in) pots, grown on and hardened off, before planting out.

Recommended plants

Argyranthemum 'Jamaica Primrose': yellow flowers: 'Mary Wootton': double white flowers with pink centre; *A. gracile* 'Chelsea Girl': white flowers with a yellow eye.
Bidens aurea: small yellow flowers; good as ground cover or in a hanging basket.
Calceolaria 'Kentish Hero': bronzy orange flowers in late summer.

Cheiranthus cheiri 'Harpur Crewe': yellow double flowers.
Convolvulus sabatius: good for using in hanging baskets; blue flowers.
Diascia barberae 'Ruby Field': low-growing plant with pink flowers.
Diascia rigescens: coarser foliage; pink flowers.
Diascia vigilis: strong growing with pink flowers; will sometimes over-winter outdoors.
Epilobium canum (syn. *Zauschneria californica*) 'Solidarity Pink': pink flowers.
Erysimum (syn. *Cheiranthus*) 'Bowles' Mauve': mauve flowers.
Erysimum linifolium 'Variegatum' (syn. *Cheiranthus linifolius* 'Variegatus'): variegated foliage; mauve flowers.
Fuchsia magellanica 'Alba Aureovariegata': white flowers; golden variegation; *F. magellanica molinae* 'Sharpitor': pink flowers; white variegation.
Gazania 'Cookei': mahogany flowers; grey foliage. 'Cream Beauty': cream flowers; grey-green foliage; 'Yellow Buttons': yellow double flowers; green foliage.
Hebe × *andersonii*: lilac flowers; green foliage.
Hebe ochracea 'James Stirling': white flowers; bronze foliage.
Hebe rakaiensis: white flowers.

Osteospermum *'Pink Whirls', a summer-flowering tender perennial, is best propagated and over-wintered in the cool glasshouse from cuttings taken in late summer.*

Lavatera olbia 'Rosea': bright pink flowers.

Lavatera thuringiaca 'Barnsley': white flowers with a red eye.

Lotus berthelotii: red flowers; silver foliage; ideal for hanging baskets.

Osteospermum 'Buttermilk': pale yellow flowers; 'Cannington Roy': white and purple flowers; 'Pink Whirls': pink flowers; spooned petals; 'Whirligig': blue-white flowers; spooned petals.

Pelargonium 'Citriodorum': lemon-scented foliage.

Pelargonium × fragrans 'Variegatum': pale pink flowers; small variegated foliage.

Pelargonium 'Splendide': carmine and buff flowers.

Penstemon 'Apple Blossom': blush-pink flowers; 'Firebird': bright red flowers; 'Garnet': wine-red flowers; 'Snow Storm': white flowers; 'Sour Grapes': green-blue flowers.

Salvia argentea: pinkish white flowers.

Salvia lavandulifolia: violet flowers.

Salvia uliginosa: sky-blue flowers.

Verbena: good trailing plant; 'Lawrence Johnston': red flowers; 'Sissinghurst': bright red flowers.

Bedding plants

These are expensive to buy and relatively poor value since they give only one season's display. For this reason the glasshouse owner who raises his own bedding plants can save a great deal of money.

Today most bedding plants can be raised from seed, which avoids the need for over-wintering rooted cuttings or keeping stock plants for spring cuttings. However, many attractive fuchsia and pelargonium cultivars can be raised only from cuttings. These are taken in late summer and over-wintered in a heated glasshouse. Alternatively, stock plants may be lifted from the garden, potted, over-wintered in a frost-free place (a window sill will be sufficient if a heated glasshouse is not available) and cuttings taken in spring.

Seed for bedding plants will require a germination temperature of 18–24°C (65–75°F), which is best provided by a heated propagator. Minimum glasshouse temperatures of 13–15°C (55–60°F) will be enough to grow on most bedding plants after pricking out. Bedding plants grow rapidly in soilless composts which contain a good balance of air and water but additional regular feeds will be necessary, and it is vital that plants are well-watered prior to planting out. Plants grown in soil-based composts tend to develop more slowly but ultimately make tougher plants.

If you cannot provide warm conditions for seed sowing, it is possible to buy seedlings in compost plugs which are just ready for potting on. Although more expensive than seed, they do save time and propagation space.

To grow good quality bedding plants, it is important to follow the principles of cultivation described in the chapter on running your glasshouse (see page 37), as they are quick-growing, light-demanding plants that need frequent spacing to prevent them from becoming drawn and lanky. Plants planted directly into the garden from a glasshouse will suffer a check in growth and sulk for a few weeks. Harden them off properly in a closed cold frame three to four weeks before planting out. Ventilate the frames more freely each day until the lights can be left off altogether during the day and night. Plants put out into cold frames when there is still a danger of frost will need the lights closed and an old carpet rolled over the frame at night to keep the frost out.

Recommended plants

Ageratum F₁ 'Blue Danube', F₁ 'Blue Mink', 'Tall Blue': sow from mid-winter; prick out after 4 weeks; 12 weeks from sowing to planting.

Alyssum maritimum (syn. *Lobularia maritima*) 'Rosie O'Day', 'Snowdrift', 'Wonderland': sow from mid-winter; prick out 3–4 weeks after sowing.

Antirrhinum majus (snapdragon) Coronette Series, 'Leonard Sutton', Sweetheart Mixed: sow mid- to late winter to flower in late summer in the garden.

Begonia (tuberous) Fiesta Mixed (multiflora double), F₁ Nonstop Mixed, 'Pavilion': sow from early winter; prick out after 6–8 weeks; grow on at 18–20°C (65–68°F); flowers 19 weeks after sowing.

Begonia semperflorens Options Mixed: sow early winter to early spring; prick out when large enough to handle (approximately 6 weeks); grow on at 18–20°C (65–68°F).

Cuphea ignea
The cigar plant is grown for its tubular flowers which are made up of a scarlet tube with a florid mouth marked in black and white and, which the common name suggests, resemble a lit cigar. It is a small shrubby plant (up to 30cm/1ft high) and best treated as an annual and raised each year from seed sown in late spring. Its adaptability makes it suitable for bedding out in the summer garden, displayed in mixed hanging baskets or equally well combined with other flowering pot plants on the glasshouse bench.

The everlasting strawflower Helichrysum bracteatum 'Bright Bikini' makes an attractive pot-grown plant, flowering in the cool glasshouse in spring from a late summer sowing, or it can be planted out in the garden in early summer. Flowering is extended by dead-heading.

Callistephus chinensis (china aster) 'Comet', Pinocchio Mixed, Pompon Splendid Mixed: sow early to mid-spring at 15–20°C (60–68°F) for planting out in late spring to early summer.

Dahlia 'Figaro', Showpiece Hybrids Mixed: sow late winter to mid-spring at 15–20°C (60–68°F); plant out in early summer; plants can be used the following year by saving the tubers.

Dorotheanthus bellidiflorus (syn. *Mesembryanthemum criniflorum*) 'Lunette', Magic Carpet Mixed: sow late winter to early spring; cover seed at 15–18°C (60–65°F); germinates in 10–14 days.

Gazania × hybrida Harlequin Hybrids: sow late winter to early spring at 15–20°C (60–68°F); plant out in sunny position from early summer; full germination takes 21 days.

Helichrysum bracteatum 'Bright Bikini', 'Hot Bikini': sow in mid- to late spring at 15–20°C (60–68°F) for flowering in the summer flower garden; if sown in late summer and grown in pots in the cool glasshouse

over winter, will flower under glass in spring.

Impatiens (busy lizzie) 'Double Confection', Super Elfin, Tempo Mixed: sow early to mid-spring at 15–20°C (60–68°F) in a soilless compost mix; cover with polythene until germination for optimum results.

Ipomoea tricolor 'Heavenly Blue': soak seed prior to sowing at 15–20°C (60–68°F) in mid- to late spring for planting out in early summer.

Limonium sinuatum (statice) Fortress Mixed: sow in early spring at 19–20°C (66–68°F); prick out into trays for planting out in late spring.

Lobelia erinus 'Blue Cascade', 'Crystal Palace': sow mid-winter to early spring at 15–20°C (60–68°F) on the compost surface; prick out into trays.

Nemesia strumosa 'Blue Gem', Carnival Mixed, 'Tapestry': sow mid-winter to early spring at 15–20°C (60–68°F); cover seed and prick out soon after germination into cell or unit pots as plant resents disturbance.

Pelargonium (zonal) F_1 'Apple Blossom Orbit', F_1 'Startel', F_1 Video Series Mixed: sow mid- to late winter at 21–24°C (70–75°F) for planting out in early summer; prick out into peat pots.

Petunia × hybrida Super Magic Series, 'Telstar', F_1 Victorious Double Mixed: sow early spring at 18–25°C (65–77°F); do not cover seed with compost; prick out when large enough to handle.

Salvia splendens 'Carabiniere', 'Firecracker': sow late winter to mid-spring at 19–25°C (66–77°F) cover seed; germination can take up to 21 days.

Tagetes erecta (african marigold) F_1 Inca Mixed, F_1 'Orange Jubilee', F_1 Perfection Series: sow in mid-spring at 20–25°C (68–77°F); prick out and grow on in trays at 12–16°C (54–61°F).

Tagetes patula (french marigold) 'Queen Sophia', F_1 'Seven Star Red', F_1 'Solar Gold': as for *T. erecta*.

Verbena hybrida 'Showtime', 'Springtime': sow mid-winter to early spring at 15–20°C (60–68°F); germination takes 2–3 weeks; prick out into trays and grow on at 13°C (55°F).

Viola × wittrockiana (pansy) F_2 'Jolly Joker', Roggli Giant Mixed, F_1 'Universal': sow in early summer for winter and spring flowering; sow in mid-winter for flowering in spring and early summer; germinate at 15–18°C (60–65°F).

Edible crops

In addition to the many ornamental plants, there is a wide variety of fruit and vegetables – exotic and out-of-season – that can be raised successfully in the glasshouse to support the kitchen garden.

Tomatoes

In warm countries tomatoes may be cropped all year round without protection but in cooler regions, such as northern Europe, year-round cropping can be achieved only in a glasshouse environment. The flavour of freshly picked, home-produced tomatoes has made them one of the most popular summer glasshouse crops for many gardeners.

Crop timetable

For an early summer crop, sow the tomato seed in a heated glasshouse between early to mid-winter, planting out in late winter to early spring. The disadvantage of this early crop is that much valuable glasshouse space is taken up at a time when it is in greatest demand for propagating bedding plants for the garden. For this reason most gardeners sow in late winter or early spring, planting out in mid- to late spring, with the first fruit being ready for harvesting in mid-summer.

Sowing

Sow tomato seed thinly in pots or trays in a seed compost and give a light covering of compost before watering in. The seed is best germinated in a propagator where a minimum temperature of 18°C (65°F) can be maintained.

Pricking out

The seed should germinate in 8–11 days and can be pricked out into a sterilized potting compost in 11cm (4¼in) pots when the seedling leaves are fully expanded. If only a few tomato plants are needed, sow two seeds directly into 11cm (4¼in) peat pots, removing the weaker seedling after germination. Tomatoes often have a long seedling stem, so, when pricking out, make sure that the hole you make with

the dibber is deep enough for the root and seedling stem to be inserted in the compost, leaving the seed leaves just above the soil surface.

Growing on

The newly-potted seedlings should then be placed on the glasshouse bench with the pots touching. They need to be protected from direct sunlight for a couple of days until the seedlings have established. As the tomato plants grow they must be spaced so that the leaves of adjoining plants do not touch to prevent overcrowding. Plants must not be allowed to dry out or become over-watered as this will seriously affect healthy development. Water requirement will vary depending on the compost, glasshouse temperature and prevailing weather conditions. However, rapidly-growing young plants will need checking for watering at least once a day. To ensure a balanced development, temperatures at this stage in the plant's development should not be allowed to drop

These tomatoes were planted in their final position in a growing bag when flowers showed on the first truss. Established plants require watering more than once a day during warm weather, and plants grown in coir-based composts will dry out quicker than those in peat-based composts.

below 16°C (61°F) at night or exceed 21–23°C (70–73°F) during the day. Constant manual supervision of the temperature will be unnecessary if you have an automatic ventilator.

Planting out

If the border soil is to be used, it should be dug over in winter and organic matter such as peat and well-rotted manure added. A general base fertilizer with an N:P:K ratio of 1:1:1 should be applied and raked in prior to planting. Tomatoes can only be grown in the glasshouse border for a couple of seasons before the quality of the plants starts to decline due to a build-up of specific pests and diseases such as tobacco mosaic virus (see page 57) and fruit and stem rot (see page 68). Although the soil in the border can be dug out to a depth of 30cm (1ft) and replaced with sterilized potting compost, it is a time-consuming and expensive process.

Tomatoes are ready for planting out when the flower on the first truss (lowest and first-formed cluster of flowers) opens. Pot each plant into a 23cm (9in) pot or polythene bag pot with a sterilized potting compost and water in well. The pots should be spaced 45–60cm (1½ft–2ft) apart on a polythene or gravel base. If you are using growing bags, first cut out the panels in the top of the bag and make slits in the sides for drainage. Then, loosen up the compost and water thoroughly before planting the tomato plants 45cm (1½ft) apart. Particular care must be taken to ensure that all the compost is thoroughly moistened.

Aftercare

Once the roots have filled the container, the plants will need regular watering, as much as twice a day during the height of the summer. Tomatoes should never be allowed to dry out as this will cause the fruit to go brown at the base – this is commonly referred to as blossom end rot – and irregular watering can cause the fruit to split. To avoid temperatures over 30°C (86°F) the glasshouse should be shaded and well-ventilated in hot weather. Damping the glasshouse floor and foliage will help to reduce temperatures and increase humidity which in turn aids pollination and fertilization.

Feeding

Tomatoes are avid feeders and should be given a dilute liquid feed at most waterings. A high potash feed with an N:P:K ratio of 1:0:3 is required early in the growing season – from potting until fruit starts to appear on the first truss – to prevent over vigorous growth; the main feed should have a balance between nitrogen and potash of 2:1:4, and when the plant has reached its full size a higher nitrogen liquid feed with an N:P:K ratio of 1:1:1 can be used to maintain vigour. However, many gardeners produce good crops by using a high potash liquid tomato feed only. It is a good idea to flush the compost through with water to prevent an excessive build-up of nutrients, especially in peat-based compost. Plants that are dry or wilting should not be fed until the compost is properly moistened as a sudden influx of nutrients on dry compost can rapidly increase the salt content of the compost, damaging plant roots.

Training

Tomatoes under glass are best grown on single stems (cordons) as this makes management and picking easier. All side shoots which develop between leaf and stem should be removed by pinching out as they appear but take care not to remove any flower trusses! If grown in the glasshouse border, the plants may be tied with soft string to a bamboo cane for support. Another method is to tie one end of a piece of 5-ply string loosely below the lower leaves of the plant and tie the other end to a horizontal wire supported by the glasshouse roof 1.8–2.5m (6–8ft) above ground level. As the plant grows, wind it around the string to keep it upright. For plants grown in bags, it is advisable to place purpose-built wire frames over the bags to support bamboo canes to which the tomato plants can be tied.

For most cultivars grown on the single stem system the main growth should be stopped (pinched out) two leaves after the fifth flower truss. Yellowed lower leaves up to the first truss can be removed to help improve air circulation.

Where glasshouse space is limited, bush tomatoes, which form low, multi-stemmed plants and require no training or tying, are most suitable. As the fruits are produced at ground level, mulch with

'Gardener's Delight'
These delicious cherry tomatoes are perfect whole in salads or for eating straight from the plant! The name tomato originates from the Aztec word tomatl, *and the tomato we grow today originates from two South American plants,* Lycopersicon lycopersicum *and* L. pimpinellifolium. *Tomatoes were first grown in Europe as ornamental plants rather than for their fruits which were thought to be poisonous.*

RIGHT *This mature tomato plant has had its leading shoot pinched out just before reaching the glasshouse roof. The leading shoots of cordon-trained plants are usually pinched out two leaves after the fifth flower truss, and lateral shoots are removed as soon as they appear.*

black polythene or straw to keep them off the soil and prevent them from rotting.

Pollination

Although tomatoes are self-pollinating, they can be encouraged to release pollen by tapping the supporting wires or canes. Damping the plants up to three times on a warm sunny day will create the ideal conditions for fertilization. Take care not to damp down on dull or overcast days as too high a humidity will encourage fungal disorders.

Harvesting

Fruits should be picked when they are ripe and fully coloured. Snap the swollen portion of the flower stalk, leaving the green calyx attached to the fruit. If there are still unripe fruit at the end of the season, remove them and place in a large can or empty drawer with a couple of ripe apples. The apples will give off ethylene gas that will help the green tomatoes to ripen.

Old tomato plants should be removed from the glasshouse and burnt to avoid the carrying-over of pests and diseases. The compost in the peat bags or pots can be used to mulch the vegetable garden.

Recommended cultivars

Standard tomatoes – 'Ailsa Craig': popular tomato with medium-sized fruit; grown for flavour; 'Alicante': reliable crop of good flavoured fruit; resistant to greenback; F_1 'Grenadier': fine crop of large fruit; resistant to greenback and tomato leaf mould; F_1 'Herald': fine flavour; resistant to greenback; F_1 'Shirley': early cropper; resistant to tobacco mosaic virus, tomato leaf mould and greenback; F_1 'Supercross': good cropper; resistant to tobacco mosaic virus, tomato leaf mould and greenback.

Beefsteak tomatoes – 'Big Boy': large, fleshy fruit; 'Dombello': early variety; large, fleshy fruit; resistant to a number of diseases.

Novelty tomatoes – 'Golden Sunrise': early maturing; sweet, yellow fruit; 'Tangella': unusual orange fruit; ripens early; resistant to greenback; 'Tigerella': yellow- and red-striped fruit; good flavour.

Cherry tomatoes – 'Gardener's Delight': one of the most popular cherry tomatoes due to its heavy yields and good flavour; F_1 'Sweet 100': similar to 'Gardener's Delight'; good cropper.

Bush tomatoes – 'Red Alert': early cropper with small fruit; good flavour; F_1 'Sigma Bush': open growth helps fruit to ripen; early, good quality cropper; F_1 'Totem': good crop; good resistance to disease; suitable for window boxes.

Pests and diseases

Apart from problems with general glasshouse pests such as whitefly and red spider mite (see page 57), there are a number of problems particular to growing tomatoes. However, modern F_1 tomato hybrids are resistant to many diseases and pests, including tobacco mosaic virus (see page 57) and potato cyst eelworm. If problems occur, resistant cultivars should be selected from seed catalogues. However, it is always advisable to grow plants each year in fresh, sterilized compost and make sure that any tools you use are cleaned thoroughly between each crop to prevent any carry-over disease.

Blossom end rot: A hard, dark brown, leathery area forms at the blossom end (base) of the fruit. It occurs most often on growing bag and container-grown plants that are allowed to dry out as the fruits are swelling.

Control: Never allow plants to dry out at the root.

Fruit and stem rot: Occurs on mature plants where a brown-black canker appears on the base of the stem, causing the leaves to become yellow and sunken. The fruit may also become infected and develop a black rot.

Control: Scrub and wash down the glasshouse and all tools and pots. Use only sterilized compost.

Greenback: The top of the fruit remains green. Cultivars such as 'Ailsa Craig' are susceptible.

Control: Caused by too much defoliation, lack of potash or an excess of sunlight. Can be avoided by not removing the lower foliage, giving a feed of high potash and increasing the shading. Many new cultivars are resistant to greenback.

Potato cyst eelworm: Produces small white cysts on roots and the root knot eelworm causes the roots to form large brown swellings. Plants wilt and become stunted with discoloured foliage.

Control: Infected plants must be destroyed and no

member of the Solanaceae (potato and tomato family) should be grown in the soil for at least six years. Use growing bags or containers instead.

Tomato leaf mould: Appears as pale yellow patches on the upper leaf surface with pale brown spores on the underside.

Control: As with most fungal diseases, spores germinate in humid conditions. Improved ventilation will increase air circulation and reduce humidity. Many modern cultivars are resistant to strains of this disease and should be used if tomato leaf mould has been a problem in the past. If the symptoms occur, spray with a suitable fungicide.

Cucumbers

Cucumbers (and melons) belong to the Cucurbitaceae, a family that also includes squashes, marrows and pumpkins.

The cucumber (*Cucumis sativus*) is most suitable as a spring and summer crop for the small glasshouse as it requires a minimum temperature of 19°C (66°F) for optimum growth which would be expensive to maintain during the colder months.

Cucumbers grow well in growing bags but need a framework for climbing. Special, free-standing tubular frames are available to which wires or strings can be attached.

Crop timetable

Sowings in mid-autumn will give croppings from late winter to early spring but these will only give good crops in areas with good winter light or if artificial lighting is used. Seed sown from mid-winter will provide cucumbers for cutting from early summer onwards. For the owner of the mixed glasshouse used primarily for spring propagation, it is best to sow cucumber seed in late winter to early spring, planting out in late spring, when most of the other plants are being hardened off. Cropping should start from mid-summer and continue until mid-autumn. Early cucumbers can be grown in a heated frame and from early summer onwards they can be planted out in a cold frame.

Sowing

Sow seed individually into seed or multi-purpose compost in 8cm (3in) pots. Press the seed into the compost so that it is 1cm (½in) below the surface. After watering in, place the seed pots in a propagator, or on a warm bench and cover over with black polythene where a temperature of 26°C (80°F) can be maintained (see page 39). Remove the polythene as soon as germination starts which will be in a couple of days. Germination will occur at lower temperatures but it takes longer and the quality of the plants is not so reliable.

Once germination is complete the seedlings should be hardened off by increasing the ventilation in the propagator. After a couple of weeks the seedlings will be ready to pot on into larger 11cm (4¼in) pots. Use a soil-based potting compost (such as John Innes No. 2) or soilless alternative, taking great care not to damage any roots. After potting, insert a 45cm (1½ft) split cane into the pot and tie the growing stem (not too tightly) to the cane with soft string. To avoid potting on and possible root disturbance, you can sow the seed directly into 11cm (4¼in) pots but take great care not to overwater at the early stages of growth.

Cucumbers like a humid atmosphere, and the glasshouse floor should be damped down regularly and shading used from mid-spring onwards, or earlier during bright seasons, and ventilation given to prevent overheating.

Planting

Cucumbers may be planted out when they have eight to ten leaves. If planting into the glasshouse border, the cucumbers will benefit if the level of the soil is raised to ensure good drainage. Organic matter in the form of well-rotted manure, with a good straw content should be dug in at least two weeks before planting and a base fertilizer applied. As with tomatoes, pests and diseases build up if cucumbers are grown in the same soil each year. Many cucumber growers find that their plants grow equally well planted either in 25cm (10in) pots in a soil-based compost (such as John Innes No. 3) or a soilless alternative, or in a growing bag shared between two plants. These alternative methods of planting also allow a more flexible use of the glasshouse space.

Spacing

Cucumbers should be spaced 60cm (2ft) apart and staked to support the plants. It is also possible to train them up horizontal wires or trellis, as described for melons on page 71.

Feeding

Plants in containers should be fed with a tomato fertilizer every one to two weeks. Bed-raised cucumbers can be mulched once surface roots are observed, which prevents capping (compaction of the soil) and assists good air movement through the soil. A well-rotted manure or a soil-based compost (such as John Innes No. 3) are good alternatives for mulching but make sure the manure is not too strong otherwise it can scorch the roots.

Training

Cucumbers, like tomatoes, are most easily grown on single stems (cordons) which are tied in to a vertical cane or horizontal wires. The wires are spaced 20cm (8in) apart on the glasshouse wall and roof. The growing point of the leading stem will need to be pinched out when it reaches the glasshouse roof. Side shoots are pinched out two leaves beyond the female flower – identified by the immature cucumber behind it. Male flowers have only a thin stalk behind the flower and should be removed on ordinary cucumber cultivars to prevent pollination as fert-

Cucumbers grow rapidly and need the support of wires or other framework to which the stems are tied with soft string. Regular harvesting should ensure successive supplies of fruit.

ilized fruit has a bitter taste and is misshapen. Modern, all-female cultivars of cucumber are available which save the job of removing male flowers. They are also more resistant to disease but tend to produce shorter fruit.

Harvesting

Full-sized fruit should be removed by cutting the stalk with a sharp knife or secateurs, taking care not to damage the main stalk. If the cucumbers are left on the plant to turn yellow, the plant will cease producing fruit.

Recommended cultivars

Traditional – 'Conqueror': good flavour; suitable for a cold glasshouse; 'Telegraph': long fruit.

All-female F_1 cultivars – 'Birgit': consistent, large, slightly ribbed fruit; resistant to gummosis; 'Carmen': good crops; resistant to powdery mildew; 'Fembaby': small plant with small fruits; easy to train; 'Pepinex 69': yields well; resistant to gummosis; 'Petita': easily grown; produces many short fruits; resistant to gummosis.

Pests and diseases

Many of the fungal disorders suffered by cucumbers (and melons) are caused by poor ventilation and unsterilized compost and pots. Reusing old compost and dirty pots allows pests and diseases to be carried over from crop to crop.

Anthracnose: First appears as pale green, sunken spots towards the blossom end of the fruit which then turn pink and are covered with mould which in turn becomes black and powdery. Fruit eventually yellows and dies.

Control: Remove and destroy infected fruit. Treat with a suitable fungicidal powder. Ventilate adequately and use sterilized compost and equipment before each crop.

Cucumber mosaic virus: Causes yellow and green mottling on the foliage and misshapen fruit which develop dark green warts.

Control: Spread by aphids. If aphids are present, apply a suitable, non-persistent insecticide. Destroy infected plants. Wash hands and tools to prevent further spread via infected sap.

Gummosis: Sunken spots on fruit which ooze a treacle-like gum, later developing a dark mould.

Control: Disease is encouraged by cool, moist conditions. Improve the growing environment by raising the temperature and increasing ventilation to reduce humidity. Destroy any infected fruit and spray with a suitable fungicide. Grow resistant cultivars in future.

Potato cyst eelworm: See page 68.

Powdery mildew: Can be a serious problem with cucumbers. See page 57.

Control: Use resistant cultivars. Prevent plants drying out at the root and ventilate well.

Melons

Melons (*Cucumis melo*) are grown for the sweet flesh of their fruit. Although they will produce fruit at any time of the year, those that mature during short winter days take a long time to ripen and are of insufficient quality to make them worthwhile. If a long season of cropping is required, first sow in early winter for the first crop to mature in late spring, and at intervals from mid-winter to produce fruit 16–20 weeks later. Seed for the latest advisable crop should be sown in mid-summer to produce fruit ready for cutting between late autumn and early winter. If you wish to grow melons in a frame or unheated glasshouse, seed should be sown in early to mid-spring, planted out in the frame or unheated glasshouse in mid- to late spring and harvested in late summer and early autumn.

Sowing
Seed should be sown and treated in the same way as cucumber seed (see page 69), but germination is improved if it is inserted in the compost either on its side or pointed end down.

Planting
Treat as for cucumbers but special care must be taken not to let plants dry out at any time, as melons have a high water requirement and insufficient water produces undersized, poorly flavoured fruits that are liable to split. However, too much water will lead to problems with diseases.

Feeding
As for cucumbers (see page 69).

Training
Melons need frequent attention and can be tied either to horizontal wires spaced 20cm (8in) apart or to some form of trellis work. The main shoot should be trained upright to a height of 120cm (4ft) and then pinched out. Lateral shoots bearing fruit are stopped at four leaves beyond the fruit; all other laterals and sub-laterals are stopped after one leaf or removed to prevent overcrowding. Melons develop rapidly during their growing season. It is therefore advisable to train and tie in the shoots daily.

Pollination
The female flowers need to be pollinated by hand otherwise the fruit will remain small. This is done by removing a male flower, pulling off the surrounding petals and lightly pressing it into the centre of the female flowers (you can distinguish them by a swelling behind the female flower). Pollination should be carried out when the sun is shining and

five or six flowers on each plant should be pollinated at a time to ensure a consistent development of all the fruit. Damping down the floor of the glasshouse after pollination will increase humidity which aids fertilization. As the melons develop, they must be supported in a net which is attached to the support wires or trellis, otherwise they may tear themselves from the mother plant.

Harvesting
Fruits must remain on the plant until they are fully coloured, which indicates that the full flavour has developed. A fruit is usually ready to cut when there is a slight cracking around its stem.

Recommended cultivars
Canteloupe types (rounded fruits often with white netted skins) – 'Ogen': green flesh; 'Romeo': small fruit with good flavour; good late cropper; suitable for cold summer growing; 'Sweetheart': good flavour; scarlet flesh; suitable for summer growing in cold glasshouse or frame; 'Tiger': early maturing; orange flesh.

It is important to support the weight of developing melons. Here, netting is used to prevent the fruits tearing from the plant before they ripen. Regular watering is essential for the fruits to swell.

Casaba types (large, oval fruits with green, finely ridged skins) – 'Blenheim Orange': old cultivar still popular; orange flesh; good flavour; 'Hero of Lockhinge': traditional cultivar with white flesh; 'Honeydew': good flavoured fruit; white flesh.

Pests and diseases
As for cucumbers (see page 70).

Lettuces

Lettuces are a rewarding crop to grow in frames, or cold or cool glasshouse conditions for harvesting from early winter through to late spring. If there is not enough space available for growing them under glass in winter, young plants can be raised from seed sown in late winter and planted out in unheated frames or under cloches in the open ground in early spring. Harvesting will then take place from late spring through to early summer.

Sowing
Lettuces may be sown in pots and, after germination, pricked out into boxes and planted out into the border or growing bags when approximately 4cm (1½in) tall. Multi-unit trays or peat blocks are now very popular for sowing lettuces with three seeds sown per cell. After germination you need to remove the two weaker seedlings from each cell. This method of sowing reduces the handling of, and possible damage to, the delicate young lettuce plants as they can be planted straight out from the cells to their final growing position.

Planting
Plant the lettuces 15–30cm (6–12in) apart, directly into the glasshouse border, irrigating the beds well before planting. Alternatively, they can be planted in growing bags previously used for tomato or cucumber crops. When preparing the old bags, remove any large roots from the previous crop and flush the bags through with water two or three times to remove any excess fertilizer salts that may have built up over the previous growing season. Between eight to ten lettuce plants can be accommodated in each growing bag.

Aftercare
Plants will need regular watering once temperatures start to rise in the late winter. This is best carried out in the morning or early afternoon to allow excess moisture to dissipate before nightfall as moisture lying on the foliage will encourage disease. Ventilate once the outside temperatures are above 7–10°C (45–50°F). This is especially important after watering, when the humidity is high. Feeding should take place weekly with a high potash liquid feed (1:0:2) once the plants start to grow in spring.

Harvesting
Lettuces are ready for cutting once the head has formed. It is a good idea to start cutting the first plants just before they are fully mature to spread out the harvesting period.

Recommended cultivars
Butterhead – 'Cynthia': quick to mature; good quality and flavour; 'Kloek': solid hearts; good for a mid-winter crop; 'Kweik': very quick to mature; good strong flavour.
Crisphead – 'Kelly': slow to mature; good quality and flavour; 'Marmer': short day, 'Iceberg' lettuce.
Loose leaf – 'Novita': quick to mature; good appearance and flavour.

Pests and diseases
The main problems are aphids which can be controlled with a non-persistent insecticide, and downy mildew (see page 57).

CROP TIMETABLE		
Heated glasshouse (7°C/45°F)		
SOWING	PLANTING	HARVESTING
Early autumn	Mid-autumn	Early winter
Mid-autumn	Late autumn	Late winter
Late autumn	Early winter	Early spring
Early winter	Mid-winter	Mid-spring
Unheated glasshouse		
SOWING	PLANTING	HARVESTING
Early/Mid-autumn	Early/Mid-winter	Early/Mid-spring
Mid-autumn	Mid-/Late winter	Mid-spring
Mid-/Late autumn	Late winter	Mid-/Late spring
Cold frame		
SOWING UNDER GLASS	PLANTING	HARVESTING
Mid-winter	Late winter	Mid-/Late spring
Late winter	Early spring	Late spring

This chart of the sowing, planting and harvesting times of lettuce shows the seasonal adaptability of this crop when grown under glass.

Aubergines (egg plants)

Sow aubergines in late winter to early spring, using the methods described for lettuces (see page 72), but provide germination temperatures of 20–25°C (68–77°F), reducing to 15–18°C (60–65°F) after germination. Potted on in soil-based compost (such as John Innes No. 2) or equivalent soilless compost until they reach 23cm (9in) pots. Alternatively raise three plants per growing bag.

Aftercare and training

Stake each plant for support and pinch out the growing point when the plant reaches 30cm (1ft) in height. Damp the plant over in warm weather to encourage the fruit to set. Once five fruits have formed, remove any lateral shoots and remaining flowers. It is important to water the plants regularly and once the aubergines begin to swell, feed with a tomato fertilizer at each watering.

Harvesting

The fruits may be cut off once they have reached their full size and while they are still shiny. Older, dull fruit tends to be overripe and bitter.

Recommended cultivars

'Black Prince': large, dark fruit; 'Easter Egg': small, egg-shaped fruit; 'Elondo': resistant to mosaic virus; 'Little Fingers': small, long fruit; good yield.

Pests and diseases

Red spider mite may be a problem with this crop but can be reduced by damping down in warm weather. Aphids and whitefly may also occur and for their control see page 57.

Peppers

Both sweet and chilli peppers may be grown using the same methods as described for aubergines. Sweet peppers are available in a number of colours, from the more common green and red to yellow, orange and purple.

Chilli peppers produce tall plants up to 1.5m (5ft) high and will require the support of canes and

strings, the tallest cultivars with larger fruits needing frequent tying in to keep the plants tidy. If you have an abundant crop, some fruits may be dried after harvesting by threading them on to a string, which can be hung up in the kitchen.

Recommended cultivars

Sweet peppers – 'Ariane': fast-growing; good sized, orange fruit; 'Canape': consistent cropper; suitable for cooler conditions; ripens to red; 'Midnight Beauty': dark purple fruit; 'Redskin': red fruit; good cropper.

Chilli peppers – 'Hot Mexican': long, pointed fruit; can yield up to 33 fruits per plant; 'Red Cherry': tiny, round fruit full of seeds; produces approximately 15 fruits per plant.

Pests and diseases

Sweet and chilli peppers may suffer from whitefly, red spider mite and aphids. Refer to page 57 for their control. Incorrect watering may cause blossom end rot (see page 68).

Sweet peppers make a tasty addition to the home-grown summer salad. They can be left on the plant until they colour, or harvested early while they are still green which will encourage the development of more fruit.

Okra

Soak the okra seed in water for 24 hours before sowing. Cultivation is then similar to that for aubergines although okra is self-supporting and does not require staking. Warm conditions and ventilation during the day to reduce humidity are required. Harvest the pods from early summer to early autumn and cut three times a week to prevent them becoming too large and stringy.

Recommended cultivars

'Clemson Spineless': pale, ribbed pods; 'Green Fingers': five-sided slender pods.

Pests and diseases

Okra may suffer from aphids, whitefly and red spider mite (see page 57).

Forcing vegetables

Rhubarb, seakale, chicory, and herbs, such as parsley, mint and chives, can all be forced into growth in the heated glasshouse to be ready for harvesting from mid-winter to early spring. Rhubarb crowns should be lifted from the garden in autumn and left on the ground for a few weeks to allow frost to break dormancy. The crowns can then be potted up or placed in trays of moist peat and put under the glasshouse bench in the dark. If temperatures are kept at 18–20°C (65–68°F), you will have a very tasty crop of rhubarb in four to five weeks.

Seakale crowns should be lifted from the garden in late autumn, potted up into 15cm (6in) pots and forced in the dark under the glasshouse staging, as described for rhubarb. Pots should be forced a few at a time from late autumn to mid-winter for a supply of succulent white shoots throughout the winter. Cut off the shoots at ground level when they are 15–23cm (6–9in) long. Chicory roots over 30cm (1ft) in length should be lifted from the vegetable garden from late autumn and, after removing the leaves, potted upright into large pots or deep wooden boxes filled with old compost. They are then forced in the dark when the temperature is above 15°C (60°F). Harvest the white shoots by cutting off at ground level when they are 15–23cm (6–9in) in length.

Mint and chives are forced into growth by lifting dormant winter plants from the garden, potting up and growing in the glasshouse at temperatures above 10°C (50°F). Parsley is sown in mid- to late summer and grown in pots in the glasshouse to be ready for the kitchen in winter.

This guide to the main sowing, planting and harvesting times can be used to plan the organization of your glasshouse space.

PLANNING CHART												
	EARLY WINTER	MID-WINTER	LATE WINTER	EARLY SPRING	MID-SPRING	LATE SPRING	EARLY SUMMER	MID-SUMMER	LATE SUMMER	EARLY AUTUMN	MID-AUTUMN	LATE AUTUMN
TOMATOES	SOW		PLANT OUT					HARVEST				
			SOW		PLANT OUT				HARVEST			
CUCUMBERS			SOW			PLANT OUT			HARVEST			
MELONS				SOW								
					PLANT OUT							
									HARVEST			
LETTUCE (HEATED)											SOW	
												PLANT OUT
			HARVEST									
LETTUCE (COLD)											SOW	
		PLANT OUT			HARVEST							
AUBERGINES/PEPPERS			SOW		PLANT OUT				HARVEST			
OKRA			SOW		PLANT OUT		HARVEST					

Grapes

Although grape vines are grown successfully outdoors, variable summers can mean that a consistent crop of good quality grapes will not be guaranteed each year. Vines grown under glass can be brought into growth earlier than those outside and therefore have the advantage of a longer growing season. Vines can also be grown in pots which is particularly useful if your glasshouse space is limited and you wish to grow a variety of different fruits (see page 79).

Setting up the glasshouse

Prepare a border at least 1.5m (5ft) wide which extends the whole length of the glasshouse and to a depth of 75cm (2½ft). The vine border may be outside the glasshouse if internal glasshouse space is limited or inside which gives more control over the vines in respect to warming up the ground and watering. The vine border must be well drained. If drainage is a problem, land drains will need to be placed at the bottom of the border to allow excess water to drain away. If the border soil is poor, remove it to a depth of 30–45cm (1–1½ft) and replace it with a soil-based compost (such as John Innes No. 3). Where the border soil is of sufficient quality, it can be improved still further by adding a good fibrous, rotted manure which will increase the nutrition and structure.

Planting

Vines bought at garden centres will be two or three years old and should be planted between autumn and winter when they are dormant. Plant the vines approximately 120cm (4ft) apart in the border and spread the roots out well in the planting hole before filling in and firming. The border should then be mulched with a well-rotted manure or mushroom compost. If you are going to plant vines in the border outside, make a hole at the base of the glasshouse approximately 15cm (6in) in diameter and feed the stem through it to the inside of the glasshouse. (It is important that the hole is large enough to accommodate the stem when it is fully grown.) Pack the hole with hessian to prevent any cold air from entering the glasshouse.

Training

The main growth of the vine is best restricted to a single main stem or rod, trained from the ground up to the apex of the glasshouse. Horizontal wires are spaced 20–25cm (8–10in) apart along the side wall and roof and a minimum of 25cm (10in) away from the glass. To fix wires to wooden glasshouses, vine eyes can be screwed into the glazing bars to hold the wires; on aluminium glasshouses supports will need to be bolted to the structure; on steel glasshouses wooden battens will need to be bolted on and the vine eyes can then be screwed into them.

Immediately after planting the new vine is cut back to two buds from ground level to encourage new vigorous growth which will form the basis of a new rod. The main rod is tied in vertically to the horizontal wires and all lateral growths are tied perpendicular to the main rod. Vigorous side growths only are selected, so there is one shoot every 40cm (16in), each side of the main rod. Pinch out any other shoots after one leaf. Developing growths snap easily, so they must be tied in gradually to the wires with soft string. On mature vines each trained growth is pinched out after two leaves have formed beyond the flower clusters. Non-flowering laterals and tendrils should be pinched out after five leaves and any further growth after one leaf.

Cut bunches of grapes from the vine a couple of weeks after they have fully coloured to allow the sugars to accumulate and the flavour of the fruit to develop.

Pollination

This takes place in spring. You can help in the distribution of pollen by caressing the vine blooms. This is best done at midday, after which the glasshouse should be damped down and ventilators lowered for an hour to maintain the high humidity ideal for fertilization.

Fruit thinning

Two to three weeks after fertilization the fruits will be the size of a pea and will need their first thinning to prevent the bunches from becoming overcrowded and the grapes from splitting. To avoid bruising and marking the grapes that are to remain on the vine, use a long handled pair of scissors and small forked stick to move the fruits apart when cutting. After thinning there should be a space about the thickness of a pencil around each berry.

Pruning

Once the leaves have fallen in late autumn to early winter, you can start winter pruning. Prune back the lateral shoots to one or two buds from the main rod. These will form spur-like growths. On juvenile vines the annual growth of the main rod is cut back by two-thirds each year, until the top of the glasshouse is reached. This encourages the growth of lateral shoots. If winter pruning is left too late, sap will bleed profusely from the cut surface; although worry-ing, the flow will reduce and stop once the spring growths have developed sufficiently to take up the sap flow. After pruning peel back the loose bark from the main rod to expose sites of over-wintering pests, taking care not to damage any buds around the lateral spurs.

Vines should be given a fresh mulch of well-rotted manure or mushroom compost each winter, which should be further covered with a layer of straw to keep in the moisture.

Crop management

The glasshouse should be kept cold from late autumn through to early winter, with full ventilation to allow the vine to be fully dormant. (For earlier crops, with harvesting taking place from late summer, the glasshouse can be warmed up to 15°C (60°F) from late winter through to early spring.) From late winter, the vine rods should be lowered and supported by a long loop of string from the wire so that they are horizontal. This encourages new growths to develop evenly along the length of the rod and not just at the top. As soon as shoots have developed, retie the rod to the supporting wires. The glasshouse floor and vine rods should be damped down, ideally three times a day, to create a warm, humid atmosphere until the flowers have developed. The border should be watered regularly to supply the abundant moisture required for the surge of spring growth.

Vine training and pruning

● After planting, cut the vine back to two buds to encourage new growth (see 1, right). ● Pinch out laterals two leaves after a flower bud or after five leaves if there are no flowers (see 2, right).
● Once the leaves drop, cut back the laterals to two buds (see 3, right).

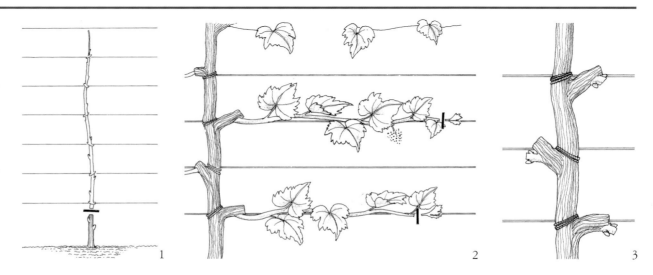

1   2   3

Harvesting

This can be from late summer through to early winter, depending on the cultivars grown and the management of the vines. Bunches of grapes should be cut from the lateral shoots with secateurs.

Recommended cultivars

Black grapes – 'Alicante': large berries; matures in late autumn; 'Black Hamburgh': one of the most popular sweet grapes; matures in early autumn; 'Black Monukka': good crop of seedless fruit in mid-autumn; 'Lady Downe's Seedling': large, oval, fine-flavoured, purple berries in late autumn; 'Muscat Hamburg': fine flavour; matures in mid-autumn.
White grapes – 'Buckland Sweetwater': large, sweet, amber berries; matures early autumn; 'Foster's Seedling': fine tasting large fruit in early autumn; 'Lady Hutt': good quality fruit with pale yellow berries produced mid- to late autumn; 'Mrs Pearson': excellent flavour; matures late autumn; 'Muscat of Alexandria': large, high-quality berries; matures mid- to late autumn.

Pests and diseases

Mealy bugs and red spider mites (see page 57) are best controlled by painting dormant rods with a suitable insecticide in winter, taking care to avoid sensitive buds. Powdery mildew (see page 57) often results from inadequate ventilation and the vines being too dry at the roots. Once the fruit is ripe, birds must be kept out of the glasshouse by netting over the ventilators. Rodents should also be controlled at this time.

Fruit in pots

Although growing fruit trained to perfection under glass is a great challenge, it does limit your time and space for growing other plants. One way of growing a great variety of different fruits in a restricted area is to grow them in pots which can then be put out on the patio during the summer.

The restricted root growth of most fruiting plants in pots means that regular watering is needed at least once a day in summer. Feeding may start in spring, with a high potash feed every two weeks, increasing

to weekly in summer. Fruiting plants are best potted in a compost containing a proportion of loam (such as John Innes No. 3), as this will give the container more stability, as well as provide a consistent supply of nutrients to the established fruit trees. Containers can be clay or plastic pots or wooden tubs. Each will grow good plants but trees planted in clay pots will need more frequent watering in summer and plastic pots are easily blown over outside in the wind. Trees may be potted up into pots ranging from 23cm (9in) to 38cm (15in), depending on the size of the original plant and available space. Trees should be potted on each year until the larger sized pot is reached. From then on they should be top-dressed each year and rejuvenated every other year in late winter (see page 49). Support each tree with a stout stake.

Correct training and thinning of shoots is important to restrict the number of bunches on the vine. Excessive vegetative growth prevents light and air from reaching the fruit, encouraging the development of powdery mildew.

Frost-hardy fruit should be left outdoors during the autumn and early winter period, so they can receive a cold treatment to break dormancy. This allows their buds to develop quickly when they are brought into the protected environment of the glasshouse in late winter. Fruit grown in pots should always have their root balls protected from frost which can penetrate the side of the pot and cause root damage. The best way of achieving this is to sink the pots in soil up to their rims in the garden in autumn before serious frosts threaten.

Virtually all fruit can be grown in pots, as long as a big enough pot can be found! I will briefly describe a few of the fruits that respond well to this treatment. Remember that large plants in clay pots filled with soil-based compost are heavy and difficult to manoeuvre.

Peaches and nectarines

The new, genetically-dwarfed cultivars of peaches and nectarines, which can bear up to 12 fruits per plant, are grown easily in pots. They need little pruning, which is restricted to cutting out any dead, diseased or damaged wood after fruiting.

As with grape vines, peaches and nectarines must be kept cold once they drop their leaves in the autumn. They are then started into growth in late winter by raising the glasshouse temperature to 10°C (50°F). The glasshouse should be well ventilated to avoid excessive temperatures until after the fruit has set when the temperatures should be increased to 18–21°C (65–70°F). The glasshouse floor should be damped down and the plants sprayed over until flowering takes place to encourage healthy growth.

Pollination Flowers are produced early in the season. To assist pollination tap the branches and brush the open flowers with some cotton wool to spread the pollen from flower to flower.

Fruit thinning Once the fruits are the size of a marble they must be thinned to one fruit per cluster. A second thinning after the natural fruit drop may be necessary to reduce the number of fruits on an overburdened tree. Use scissors to make a neat cut and avoid tearing the wood.

Harvesting Help fruits to ripen by removing leaves shading the fruit. Fruits are ripe when they are full size and part easily from the plant.

Recommended cultivars
Peaches – 'Bonanza': medium-sized fruit; yellow skin with pink blush; juicy, yellow flesh; available as short standards on 90cm (3ft) stems.
Nectarines – 'Nectarella': medium-sized fruit; green-yellow skin with pink blush; yellow flesh; available as short standards on 90cm (3ft) stems.

Pests and diseases In addition to pests and diseases common to other glasshouse plants, peaches and nectarines can suffer from the following.
Bacterial canker: Shows up as scarred wood which will eventually girdle and kill off a stem.
Control: Cut out infected portions and spray with a suitable fungicide.
Peach leaf curl: Appears as large red blisters which turn to white on the new growth in spring. This is a common problem with peaches grown outside; should not occur under glass.
Control: Treat with a suitable fungicide.
Silver leaf: Silver discoloration on the leaves and purple-brown stain on the wood.
Control: Cut out all infected shoots and treat infected trees with pellets of *Trichoderma viride*, following the manufacturer's instructions.

Figs
Figs will produce two crops per year – the first in early summer and the second in late summer to early autumn. In the autumn cut out the oldest wood and thin any weak shoots, leaving the best young branches at their full length. They can be brought into growth in late winter increasing temperatures from 13–18°C (55–65°F) and maintaining the humidity by spraying over the plant daily. The first crop of figs will swell quickly with the increased temperatures and be ready after three months in early summer. Lateral shoots produced in the summer should be shortened to five leaves and any excessive growth removed. The last crop of fruit will develop on the same shoots as the earlier crop and ripen in late summer/early autumn.

Standard vines in pots, which are particularly attractive when in fruit, are ideal for the small glasshouse where space is at a premium, and only require the support of a stout cane.

Recommended cultivars 'Bourjasotte Grise': abundant cropper; rounded fruit; good flavour; 'Figue d'Or': sweet fruit with golden skin; good quality; 'Negro Largo': large, ribbed fruit with black skin; 'Saint Johns': pale green, pear-shaped fruit with pale green skin; juicy with excellent flavour.

Pests and diseases Figs are generally trouble-free but may suffer from mealy bugs, red spider mites and aphids on new growths (see page 57).

Grapes

To train a young standard vine in a pot you will need to allow one shoot to grow up to approximately 120cm (4ft) and pinch out all the side shoots except the top three, which should be cut back to two buds after leaf fall in the autumn. Between three and five new shoots should be allowed to develop in the spring and pinched out two leaves after a flower bunch. Non-flowering shoots are pinched out after five leaves have formed and any subsequent growth after one leaf. Cultural treatments regarding watering, damping down, pollinating and thinning are the same as for grapes grown in the glasshouse border (see page 76).

For a selection of good cultivars and information on pests and diseases, see page 77.

Apricots

Apricots in pots can be trained in a pyramid or bush shape. Fruit grows on shoots produced the previous summer and on short spurs of older wood. Spurs are encouraged by summer pruning the lateral shoots after they have formed six leaves. These are then pruned back to three leaves after fruiting. When buying an apricot plant for pot culture, select one that has been grafted on to 'St Julien A', a semi-vigorous rootstock, which makes it more suitable for growing in pots.

Recommended cultivars 'Alfred': pink flushed fruit; ripens in mid- to late summer; 'Moor Park': large fruit with red flesh; ripens in late summer.

Pests and diseases As for peaches and nectarines (see page 78).

Strawberries

Young strawberry plants raised from runners the previous summer are potted into 9cm (3½in) pots and kept in an exposed cold frame until mid- to late winter. From mid-winter they are potted on into 13cm (5in) pots of soil-based or soilless compost, or planted into growing bags 20–22cm (8–8½in) apart or into a strawberry pot. The plants should be kept in a frost-free glasshouse for the first few weeks, then gradually encouraged into growth with more heat (up to 10°C/50°F). Water and liquid feed regularly to permit rapid growth. Flowers will appear in late winter to early spring and it will be essential to hand-pollinate the open flowers. Fruit should be produced in mid- to late spring.

Recommended cultivars 'Cambridge Vigour': good sized fruit in first year; good flavour; 'Hapil': large fruit; good flavour; 'Pantagruella': very early cultivar; good flavour and yield.

Pests and diseases Strawberries may suffer from aphids and powdery mildew (see page 57).

The genetically dwarfed peach cultivar 'Bonanza' is a handsome pot-grown plant when raised as a standard. The flowers make a cheerful display in spring, and delicious fruits are produced in summer.

THE DISPLAY GLASSHOUSE

The display glasshouse can be used to grow decorative plants for show in the home, conservatory, porch or section of the glasshouse. It can also become the gardener's fantasy — a tropical rain forest, arid desert, or flowering spring garden — when the garden outside is in the depth of winter, buried beneath a mound of snow.

A vivid summer display of cascading Passiflora caerulea × racemosa *is trained over wires in the roof, and pots of streptocarpus, fuchsias, pelargoniums and the trailing* Campanula isophylla *supply a mass of flower and foliage colour on the raised gravel bench.*

81

First thoughts

The major limitation when gardening under glass is space, and in the display glasshouse this is even more apparent as plants are raised and displayed in the same area. Many glasshouse owners therefore resort to growing and displaying in separate structures. The ideal set-up for this, I think, would be to have an inexpensive glasshouse for raising plants away from any permanent plantings, and a conservatory attached to the house in which to create an attractive display of flowers and foliage. A glazed porch can also be used to display flowering plants in season from the productive glasshouse.

Many people start off with a general collection of glasshouse plants, then become fascinated by a particular group such as begonias, orchids, cacti, bulbs or even carnivorous plants! Collecting specialist groups of plants becomes a passion which results in the glasshouse being filled to overflowing. There is nothing more rewarding than obtaining a new plant species or cultivar and, after discovering its needs from other gardeners and reference books, finding out for yourself how best to grow it. More often than not, a glasshouse is built before an interest is developed in a particular group of plants. Then it is much more satisfying to grow plants suited to your glasshouse, rather than struggle to raise plants that need a totally different kind of growing environment.

The variables that can be changed in the glasshouse environment are firstly light and heat – a glasshouse on an open site is exposed to the sun throughout the day and will warm up quickly, while a shady glasshouse will receive little direct sunlight, except in the early morning and late afternoon in summer. It will warm up slowly and be suitable only for shade-loving plants such as those found naturally in woodlands. Light intensity and duration can be altered by shading or artificial lighting. Shading will also lower temperatures, as will ventilation. During the winter and at night, glasshouses can be heated to raise the temperature above that outside. In summer, however, it is usually a problem keeping the glasshouse cool enough for the majority of plants.

The other important factor to consider is humidity. Plants from a forest environment, whether cool, temperate or tropical, require a high humidity as their leaves are often large and thin and dry out easily. Plants that grow naturally in the open, in particular arid desert or scrub areas, are adapted to exposure and thrive on low humidity, a lot of light and good air circulation. The best way of providing this is to position the glasshouse on an open site with plenty of ventilation.

It is quite easy to match the plants to the glasshouse when the only requirement is to grow plants, but problems arise where a conservatory is intended as a relaxation area for people as well. Then a minimum temperature of 22°C (72°F), with a comfortable maximum of 25°C (77°F) is required and a low humidity is advisable to prevent any soft furnishings from rotting. In summer the conservatory will need to be well ventilated and shaded to stop the air from becoming unbearably hot and humid.

The following plants are suitable for different glasshouse conditions:
Shady, humid and cool (4–10°C/40–50°F): tender rhododendrons, chilean bell flowers, tree and other ferns, ivies.
Shady, humid and temperate (10–15°C/50–60°F): begonias, gloxinias, streptocarpus, pileas.
Shady, humid and tropical (15–20°C/60–68°F): tropical pitcher plants, bromeliads, acalyphas, other tropical foliage plants.
Sunny and cool: some cacti, citrus fruit, hardy annuals, many South African plants (such as *Asparagus densiflorus*) and Australian plants (such as *Anigozanthos manglesii*).
Sunny and temperate: many flowering pot plants, such as fuchsias and pelargoniums, and many cacti and succulents.

Making the display

After deciding which plants you can grow in the conditions available, you need to arrange them so that they are displayed to best effect. Before you begin, it might be worthwhile visiting botanical and display gardens to see how professional gardeners display their plants, and pick up a few ideas.

It is possible under glass to create an eye-catching display of plants, such as these shown in summer, to provide interest throughout the year.

From left to right:
*Clerodendrum
   thomsoniae*
Adiantum raddianum
Tibouchina urvilleana
Streptocarpus
Brugmansia × candida
   'Knightii'
Jasminum polyanthum
Lotus berthelotii
Columnea × banksii
Bougainvillea 'Miss
   Manila'
Begonia fuchsioides
Begonia rex
Asparagus densiflorus
   'Sprengeri'

When making bench displays, group the plants according to size and habit. Tall plants with attractive foliage, such as the fern-leaved *Grevillea robusta*, can be used at the back of a bench to provide a neutral background to enhance the groups of plants at the centre of the bench which give the main stay of colour. Edges of benches can be softened with the foliage of flowering, trailing plants such as *Lotus berthelotii* with its grey leaves and red flowers. Bring colour interest to the roof of the glasshouse with clay, plastic or open wire hanging baskets of plants with trailing stems, such as *Columnea × banksii*. Alternatively you can landscape your glasshouse and plan it like a garden.

Give vertical interest with tall shrubs, such as acacias trained against wires or trelliswork; erect a pergola in a seating area to allow scented climbers, such as *Jasminum polyanthum*, to scramble and fill the air with their scent as they intermingle with the bright papery bracts of *Bougainvillea* 'Miss Manila'. Palms and foliage plants like *Schefflera actinophylla* are a good backdrop to flowering and fruiting citrus and *Lagerstroemia indica*. On the sunny side of the glasshouse use staging to raise flowering plants in pots for display or for planting in tubs on the patio.

Begonias

Begonias originate from warm temperate and tropical forests and so thrive in a glasshouse that is shady and humid. Grown for their attractive flowers and foliage, begonias are one of the most popular groups of glasshouse plants – species such as *B. semperflorens* are used in outside summer bedding schemes; *B. rex* make handsome house plants with their attractive leaf colouring and texture; and *B. × hiemalis* cultivars are sold as flowering house plants.

All begonias can be propagated from their dust-like seed which should be sown on the surface of a soilless compost. Warm, humid conditions are required for germination which should take place in two to three weeks. Prick out the seedlings into trays as soon as they are manageable for growing on. Begonias required for summer flowering should be sown in mid- to late winter. The majority of begonias may also be propagated very easily from stem cuttings, taken either in late summer or early spring, and tuberous begonias by slicing the tubers (see below) in early spring. The large-leaved *B. rex* cultivars are also propagated from leaf cuttings.

As young plants grow and develop very quickly, raise young begonia plants at least every two years as older plants can become too big for the small glasshouse and lose their vigour when they have been growing in the same pot for a number of years. Begonias are best grown in a glasshouse with a minimum winter temperature of 15°C (60°F) and shaded from direct sunlight in summer.

Begonias are divided broadly into three groups – fibrous-rooted, rhizomatous and tuberous.

Fibrous-rooted

These begonias make good, evergreen flowering pot plants, propagated from seed or stem cuttings. They can be divided further into cane-stemmed, trailing and bushy types. Cane-stemmed begonias are large plants often with attractive foliage as well as flowers. One of my favourites is *B. luxurians* with its palm-like leaves and delicate white flowers. *B. × argenteo-guttata* has olive-green leaves with silver spots and red underside, and pendulous, pink flowers. Trailing begonias are represented by *B.*

glaucophylla with glossy green leaves and scarlet flowers and the more refined *B. solananthera*, with pale green leaves and white flowers. My three favourite bushy types are *B. fuchsioides* with small green leaves and fuchsia-pink hanging flowers; *B. scharffii* with large olive-green leaves covered with a fine down and a red underside, and pale pink flowers, and *B. serratipetala* with medium-sized, olive-green and sharply toothed leaves with pink-red spots, and deep pink flowers.

Rhizomatous

These are usually low, dome-shaped plants with attractive evergreen foliage and spring flowers produced from a mass of surface stems or rhizomes. *B. rex* cultivars have large, beautifully mottled leaves. The iron cross begonia, *B. masoniana*, has puckered leaves marked with a maroon cross.

Tuberous

These are deciduous, dying down to tubers in the winter when they should be stored in dry peat, coir fibre, shredded newspaper or sawdust, in a frost-free, dry environment. Start tubers into growth in early spring by placing them hollow side up in

Begonia × tuberhybrida 'Lou-Anne' grown in a hanging basket will give a stunning display all summer as long as they are watered and fed regularly. Fading flowers and seed pods should be removed on a daily basis to maintain a long flowering period.

boxes of damp peat at 18°C (65°F). If you wish to increase your stock further, you can either sow seed from mid- to late winter or cut the tubers into sections so that each incorporates a developing growth. Once roots show, pot up into 10cm (4in) pots and feed well. Finally, pot them on, for flowering in summer, in up to a 15cm (6in) pot.

Tuberous begonias for hanging baskets produce a mass of pendulous leaves and flowers in summer. *B. sutherlandii* is conspicuous for its small but bright orange flowers which compare dramatically with the more flamboyant *B. × tuberhybrida* cultivars such as the Pendula 'Red Cascade', with its scarlet flowers. The large-flowered *B. × tuberhybrida* cultivars produce male flowers 8–15cm (3–6in) across. Selected cultivars are, however, very expensive to buy as they are much sought after by gardeners.

Pests and diseases

The most serious pest is vine weevil and the most serious disease powdery mildew (see page 57). Begonias may also be affected by the tarsonemid mite which lives and feeds inside leaf and flower buds, causing scarring, distortion, and may prevent flowers and shoots from developing. Infected plants must be destroyed to prevent further spread.

Chrysanthemums

Most cultivated chrysanthemums are florists' chrysanthemums (*Dendranthema × grandiflorum*) grown for their familiar daisy flowers available in an incredible range of colours, shapes and sizes.

Chrysanthemums are divided into groups according to their flowering time, flower shape and size. The flowering classifications are as follows: early cultivars flower before mid-autumn; mid-season cultivars flower in mid-autumn and late cultivars in late autumn and early winter. As chrysanthemum flowers are damaged by damp and frost, mid- and late season cultivars have to be brought into the protection of the glasshouse, for flowering, before frost threatens.

Single, large exhibition blooms are divided into incurved, reflexed, and intermediate chrysanthemums. Incurved have large, double, globular heads with incurved petals. Reflexed have outer petals curving outwards and intermediate have inner petals curving inwards and outer petals curving outwards. Other flower shapes include spider, spoon, anemone-centred and single.

Cascade chrysanthemums produce hundreds of small, single, double and anemone-centred flowers on long wiry stems, and can be trained and pinched into various decorative shapes while they are growing. Hardy korean chrysanthemums have small flowers and a bushy habit, whereas charm chrysanthemums make attractive, dome-shaped plants covered with small single flowers in mid-autumn.

Although chrysanthemums will flower in one season from seed sown in late winter, selected cultivars are raised from softwood basal cuttings which grow from forced stools. A stool is made up of a stem (or stems) and roots of a one year-old plant that has flowered. Where plants are grown and have flowered in pots, cut the stems down to 2.5–5cm (1–2in) above the soil level. If they have flowered in beds, they should be cut down to approximately 23cm (9in), and any large leaves or sappy growth removed at the base. The stools should then be lifted, packed into boxes, covered with soil and watered in, and kept in a well-lit, cool glasshouse or frost-free frame until they need to be forced for cuttings. This is done by raising the glasshouse temperature to 16°C (61°F) or by placing the boxes or pots on a warmed bench.

Cuttings are usually taken from early winter to early spring, depending on the cultivar and the size of plant required. Cut or snap cuttings 5–8cm (2–3in) long from the stools, remove the lower leaves and insert in a medium of equal parts peat and sharp sand. Cuttings will normally root easily and rooting hormone will not be necessary. Place in either a closed propagation environment with bottom heat to speed up rooting, or under mist.

Rooted cuttings are potted up with a soil-based compost (such as John Innes No. 2) or soilless alternative into 9cm (3½in) pots and shaded for a few days until established. When roots have filled the container, pot the plants on to a 13cm (5in) pot and line out in a cold frame. Keep the plants covered until they are established and protect them

CHRYSANTHEMUM CUTTING TIMES

Late autumn to early winter: *Specimen plants*

Early to mid-winter: *Large exhibition cultivars*

Mid-winter: *Exhibition incurved*

Late winter: *Decoratives, late-flowering singles and pompons, charms and cascades*

Very late winter and early spring: *Early flowering (outdoor) cultivars*

Mid- to late spring: *Decoratives for dwarf plants*

Early to mid-summer: *Late flowering sprays*

Charm chrysanthemums such as 'Golden Chalice' need no training as they naturally make beautiful, dome-shaped plants, covered with hundreds of small flowers in mid- to late autumn.

Chrysanthemum shapes

Incurved

Reflexed

Intermediate

Spider

from frost at night. Final potting is into a 23cm (9in) pot after which the plants should be placed outside, once any risk of frost has passed. The ground should be level and well drained, ideally topped with ash or gravel. Each plant should be staked with the stake tied to a horizontal wire stretched between two posts to give stability.

Once established in their final pots, plants grow rapidly and when it is hot and sunny, they will need watering more than once a day. Make sure that enough water is applied to soak right through the compost in the pot. Plants should be fed weekly until the roots have filled the pot when twice weekly feeds will be required. Depending on the variety and growth type, plants will also need stopping and disbudding (see below). At the end of summer, before the first frosts, plants should be brought into the glasshouse to complete their growth and flower in a drier, warmer environment – moist, humid conditions are the greatest foe of the chrysanthemum flower.

The art of chrysanthemum growing lies in learning the requirements of different cultivars – the most suitable time to take cuttings to produce the required size of flowering plant and when to stop the plant. Plants produced from late winter cuttings should have their growing tips stopped in mid-spring when they are 23cm (9in) tall, to encourage the development of side shoots to form the first crown. A second stop is given in midsummer to induce a greater number of shoots. Flowers will be produced from this second crown. Specimen plants may receive up to five stops during the growing season. Plants that are stopped twice grow to a large size and take up a lot of space in the small glasshouse. By taking cuttings in early summer and potting three rooted cuttings directly into a 23cm (9in) pot, only one stop is required in mid- to late summer. Single rooted cuttings taken a month later in mid-summer should be potted into 15cm (6in) pots and no stopping given.

Disbudding is where unwanted buds are removed from the flowering stem. A large single bloom will result if the large terminal bud is left and the side buds removed, while a spray of smaller blooms is produced if the large terminal bud is removed and the lower ones left.

Dome-shaped charm chrysanthemums make very large plants from late winter cuttings, but it is possible to produce smaller plants more suited to the small glasshouse by taking cuttings at a later date. To the surprise of many gardeners, charm chrysanthemums need no stopping or disbudding as they branch naturally.

Recommended cultivars

Charm – 'Redbreast': bright red smaller flowers; 'Ring dove': pink with white eye; almost semi-double flowers; 'Yellow Hammer': good yellow.
Spray – 'Pink Gin': deep pink; anemone-centred; 'Romark': pure white; double.
Large exhibition – 'Golden Gigantic': large re-flexed; bronze.
Exhibition – 'Dorridge Candy': large reflexed; deep candy pink; 'Fred Shoesmith': large intermediate; white with cream centre; 'Golden Lady': medium incurved; intense buttercup yellow.
Cascade – 'The Bride': many small white flowers.

Pests and diseases

Plants should be checked regularly for pests and diseases. Aphids are a constant problem on the soft growths and flower buds, as is the leaf miner which can progress rapidly through a crop (see page 57). Leaf eelworm causes yellow and brown blotches on the leaves, starting at the base of the plant, and is controlled by warm water treatment to the dormant stools. Red spider mite and whitefly can also be a problem. The two most prevalent diseases are powdery mildew (see page 57) and white rust which forms yellow spots on the upper leaf surface and buff-coloured pustules on the reverse. Both are controlled with systemic fungicides.

Cyclamen

Cyclamen persicum cultivars may be divided into two main groups – open pollinated cultivars, which make large flowering plants with beautifully marked leaves, and newer F_1 hybrids that make compact plants in a wide range of colours.

The open pollinated cultivars are sown in mid- to late autumn and require a 14-month period from sowing to flowering, whereas F_1 hybrids achieve this in ten months from a late winter to early spring sowing. Prior to sowing, the seed should be soaked in tepid water for 24 hours to soak out germination inhibitors in the seed coat. The seed is then space sown in pots, boxes or peat inserts, given a light scattering of compost and covered with a 1cm (½in) layer of perlite. The seed requires a germina-

tion temperature of 16–18°C (61–65°F) and should emerge three to four weeks after sowing. When the seed leaves are fully expanded the layer of perlite should be removed, to expose the developing corm. Once the leaves of adjoining plants touch they are ready for potting up. Cyclamen should be potted so that the top third of the corm is exposed above soil level to avoid the possibility of rotting. For the first potting they respond well if potted up into 8cm (3in) pots in a soilless compost. Cyclamen prefer growing temperatures of 17–20°C (63–68°F).

During the growing season cyclamen should be fed regularly with a high nitrogen feed with an N:P:K ratio of 2:1:1, and well-grown plants should be potted on until they reach a 13cm (5in) pot. It is important that these plants are regularly spaced and kept in a well-ventilated glasshouse – damp air will encourage grey mould which will rot the foliage and mark the flowers. It is a valuable exercise to pick over the cyclamen regularly, removing any damaged leaves and finished flowers – do this by pulling the leaf or flower stalk from the corm. This avoids leaving stubs that will become infected.

Cyclamen foliage will start to yellow in late spring when the plant should be dried off and left in a dark, dry place. In mid- to late summer it should be brought back into the light and watered

F_1 hybrid cyclamen flower over a long period, from late autumn to early spring provided damaged leaves and faded flowers are removed carefully from the plants, and temperatures are kept below 20°C (68°F).

sparingly until it starts to grow again and normal watering and feeding can resume. Where space is limited, it is much more satisfactory to raise fresh plants each year from seed.

Recommended cultivars

Open pollinated – F₁ By-Pass Mixed: large flowers in a variety of colours; F₁ 'Grandia': white frilled flowers; Scentsation Mixed: mixed colours with good fragrance; 'Victoria': ruffled white petals edged and marked in red.

Pests and diseases

Cyclamen may suffer from aphids, vine weevil and grey mould (see page 57) and tarsonemid mites (see page 85).

Fuchsias

Fuchsias are shrubby plants originally from Central and South America; they are familiar greenhouse and tub plants for summer and autumn flowering. Most fuchsias are grown for their flowers but there are a number raised for their distinctive foliage, such as *Fuchsia* 'Genii' with its golden leaves.

Bush fuchsias

Bushy plants can be propagated from cuttings in spring but if larger plants are required, take cuttings in late summer. Plants can be pinched a number of times as soon as they start to grow to make bushy plants. Alternatively, create a standard plant where the growth is borne on the top of a single bare stem by letting a single stem grow up, removing the side shoots, until the desired height of bare stem is reached. Then it can be stopped and five to six shoots allowed to grow out to make the head of the standard. For the show bench, fuchsia standards are divided into four categories: table, quarter, half and full. The bare stem height for a table standard is 25–30cm (10–12in); for a quarter standard 30–38cm (12–15in); for a half standard 45–60cm (18–24in); and for a full standard 75–108cm (30–42in). Support the stem of a standard with a stout cane, secured with two or three neat ties of raffia or soft string.

An alternative to repropagating stock each year is to over-winter plants at a minimum temperature of 4–10°C (40–50°F). This may cause them to drop their leaves but is not a problem if they are kept dry as well as cold. In spring cut the plants back to 7–10cm (2¾–4in) from the compost, increase the temperature to a minimum of 15°C (60°F) and top-dress with fresh compost. Large bushy plants will require up to a 23cm (9in) pot to maintain a summer display of flowers. Give a high nitrogen fertilizer twice a week and remove any old flowers.

Recommended cultivars 'Margaret': semi-double with crimson sepals and violet petals; 'Mission Bells': red sepals and purple petals; 'Pink Spangles': red sepals and pale pink petals; 'Snowcap': red sepals and white petals; 'Tennessee Waltz': rose-pink sepals and semi-double, lilac petals.

Trailing fuchsias

Fuchsias with lax trailing stems are most suited to growing in hanging baskets where their flowers are displayed to the full. I take cuttings from trailers in late winter, potting up rooted cuttings into 9cm (3½in) pots. When they have grown five to six

Newly potted fuchsias, grown from late summer cuttings, will make large specimen plants by the end of the summer, concealing the benching behind a mass of foliage and flowers.

leaves pinch them to encourage branching. When the roots have filled the pots, prepare the hanging basket with potting compost and plant five to six plants per 35cm (14in) diameter basket. Flowers should be produced from mid-summer. Many trailing fuchsias with their cascading growths and flowers make stunning standard plants, as long as the base stem is supported with a stout cane.

Recommended cultivars 'Annabel': white flowers; 'Eva Boerg': white sepals and purple petals; 'Marinka': red flowers and variegated foliage; 'Pink Galore': shell-pink flowers.

Pests and diseases
Fuchsias may suffer from aphids, mealy bugs, scale insects, whitefly, grey mould and rust (see page 57).

Pelargoniums

Pelargoniums, which originate from southern Africa, grow best in a well-ventilated, sunny glasshouse, with a minimum winter temperature of 10°C (50°F), although if kept very dry in winter, they will survive near frost conditions. They flourish in a wide range of composts, as long as they are well drained and do not become waterlogged. During the growing season, from spring through to the autumn, they thrive on twice-weekly feeds which allow them to develop quickly in good light. Although stock plants can be kept over winter and spring cuttings taken, I prefer to take cuttings in the late summer and over-winter young plants in 9cm (3½in) pots, which will grow quickly in the spring, making large specimen plants growing to 45cm (1½ft) and ending up in 13–15cm (5–6in) pots. Bedding cultivars of zonal pelargoniums develop rapidly, producing plants ready for planting out in early summer, from seed sown in mid-winter.

Scented-leaved pelargoniums
Some pelargonium species are grown mainly for their aromatic foliage which, if rubbed, gives off spicy scents. The following are particularly pleasing:

Regal pelargoniums make a dramatic bench display. Good top and side ventilation is essential in order to extend the life of the flowers.

P. crispum: lemon scent; also available with attractive variegated foliage; white to pink flowers with red veins; *P. odoratissimum*: velvety, hairy leaves; apple scent; white flowers with red markings; *P. quercifolium*: oak-shaped leaves with an almond scent; pink to purple flowers with purple veins; *P.* 'Royal Oak': spicy scented; oak-shaped leaves with brown markings; mauve-pink flowers; *P. tomentosum*: grey, velvety foliage; peppermint scent.

Zonal pelargoniums
Zonal pelargoniums (*P. × hortorum*) are hybrids grown for their attractive leaves marked with zones, often in different colours, and good flowers. They are in bloom from late spring to late summer as long as the faded flowers are removed regularly.

Recommended cultivars 'Caroline Schmidt': pale green foliage with white edge; double red flowers; 'Golden Harry Hieover': gold-flushed foliage; pink flowers; 'King of Denmark': green foliage with bronze zoning; semi-double salmon-pink flowers; 'Mr Henry Cox': green-centred foliage with maroon-purple band and cream edge; pink flowers.

Regal pelargoniums

Regal pelargoniums (*P.* × *domesticum*) are compact, shrubby plants with serrated edged green leaves, grown for their flamboyant flowers borne throughout the summer. As with all pelargoniums, you can extend flowering under glass by removing the old flowers to prevent seed pods forming. When in flower they require a dry atmosphere as humid conditions will encourage the flowers to damp off.

Recommended cultivars 'Autumn Festival': salmon-pink flowers with white throat; 'Aztec': bright red flowers with purple markings and white petal edges; 'Black Knight': purple flowers with white-edged petals; 'Grand Slam': rose to violet-red flowers.

Trailing pelargoniums

Trailing pelargoniums (*P. peltatum*) are ivy-leaved and available in a tremendous range of flower colours. They are perfect as hanging basket or trough plants where their cascading growth can be displayed to full effect.

Recommended cultivars 'Abel Carrière': red to purple semi-double flowers; 'L'Elégante': variegated foliage; white flowers; 'Rouletta': semi-double white flowers with red edge to petals; 'Sybil Holmes': pink double flowers; 'Tavira': rich red flowers.

Pests and diseases

Pelargoniums may suffer from aphids, whitefly, black leg and grey mould (see page 57).

Pot plants from seed

Many gardeners shy away from glasshouse gardening because of the high cost of heating and the supposed expense of buying exotic plants. This need not be so as a wide range of hardy and half-hardy annual and biennial plants can be raised from seed and grown in a cool glasshouse with a minimum temperature of 5°C (41°F) to give a stunning display throughout the year. Many plants traditionally grown as annuals for the garden can be sown

from late summer to autumn to produce early flowering, large specimen plants for glasshouse display. Sow the seed in pots or trays, then prick out directly into pots and place in a cool, light and airy position, such as a cold frame.

It is important that plants are potted on to larger pots as soon as the roots reach the side of the pot to prevent any check in growth. This means that plants are potted on every 10–15 days while in active growth. Annuals can be protected from light frost at night by covering the frame lights with matting. However, once severe frosts threaten (below −2°C/28°F), the plants should be brought in from the cold frame to a frost-free glasshouse. Ventilate the glasshouse whenever possible, but not when there is a frost, and space the plants so that each specimen receives enough light. Plants clustered together in a warm, humid glasshouse will become drawn and leggy and need frequent staking.

Further successive sowings of many annuals can take place from late winter to early summer to produce smaller plants which will flower from summer to well into the autumn months. Some of the larger plants may need staking, which should give support without being obtrusive. Vigorous plants with thick stems such as *Lavatera trimestris* need the support of a bamboo cane while the wiry stems of *Linaria maroccana* are best supported on short, twiggy hazel stems and tied in neatly with raffia.

It is always well worthwhile leafing through seed catalogues and trying out different hardy and half-hardy annuals each year to see how plants respond to pot culture.

Summer- and autumn-sown annuals

Antirrhinum majus (snapdragon): shorter bedding cultivars are more suitable for growing in pots; Coronette and Princess Series: mixed colours; sow in mid-autumn; prick out into 8cm (3in) pots; pot on up to 15cm (6in) pots; will flower in mid- to late spring.
Calceolaria × *herbeohybrida*: swollen, slipper-like flowers in many colours; 'Jewel Cluster' and Perfection Mixed: commonly grown cultivars; sow in mid-summer; slow to start growing but good plants will flower in a 13cm (5in) pot in spring.

Gerbera jamesonii 'Happipot'

The dwarf barberton daisy is an ideal pot plant which can flower all year round. The large double and semi-double, chrysanthemum-like flowers come in mixed colours. Taller flowering Gerbera cultivars are widely grown in Holland as a cut flower crop, with blooms lasting over ten days in water.

Calendula officinalis Art Shades Mixed, 'Fiesta Gitana', 'Sun Glow': cool glasshouse pot plants; sow in late summer for late winter flowering.

Cineraria × hybrida (syn. *Pericallis × hybrida*) 'Stellata' and Superb Mixed: make larger plants; daisy-like flowers in mixed colours; sow seed from mid-summer; will flower in a 13–15cm (5–6in) pot from late winter to early spring, depending on the vigour of the cultivar.

Linaria maroccana 'Fairy Bouquet': tiny spurred flowers in mixed colours; dislikes the disturbance of pricking out so best to sow a pinch of seed in early autumn in 8cm (3in) pots, pulling out all but the best seedling once germination is complete; pot on to a 10cm (4in) then a 15cm (6in) pot; mid- to late spring flowering.

Mimulus × hybridus (monkey flower): large, thirsty plants; mixed colours; sow in early autumn; best eventually potted up into 30–35cm (12–14in) hanging baskets; will need watering at least twice a day in sunny weather when in full flower from mid-spring.

Primula vulgaris and *P.* Polyanthus: wide variety of colours; sow these hybrids in mid-summer on peaty compost; keep as cool as possible throughout germination as they will not develop properly if compost temperatures are above 22°C (72°F); prick out into trays and pot on to 9cm (3½in) pots or 13cm (5in) for larger cultivars; will flower from late winter.

Primula malacoides and *P. obconica*: traditional glasshouse plants; raise in the same way as *P. vulgaris* hybrids; will flower in a 13cm (5in) pot from late winter; *P. malacoides* bears whorls of medium-sized flowers in a variety of colours; *P. obconica* has large flowers in clusters on the top of stems.

Rehmannia angulata: pink, trumpet-shaped flowers; sow in late summer for flowering in 15cm (6in) pots in late spring; grown best as an annual from seed but plants can be cut back after flowering and grown on to flower the following year.

Salpiglossis sinuata F_1 'Casino': vibrant colour range from yellow to red; sow seed in mid-autumn to produce flared, trumpet flowers in a 15cm (6in) pot in late spring; smaller, later flowering plants can be produced from a mid-winter sowing.

Schizanthus (poor man's orchid): medium-sized butterfly-shaped flowers in a variety of colours; makes a most dramatic pot plant; two good cultivars are 'Hit Parade' and the more compact 'Star Parade'; sow seed in late summer to early autumn; seedlings develop rapidly and by late autumn plants can end up in a 23cm (9in) pot, producing flowering plants in mid- to late spring over 120cm (4ft) high.

Winter- and spring-sown annuals

Browallia: attractive, blue flowers are produced from late summer through to autumn; may be sown from mid-winter to early summer to spread out the flowering period; larger plants such as 'Jingle Bells' and 'Marine Bells' will flower in a 13cm (5in) pot whereas the dwarf cultivars 'Blue Troll' and 'White Troll' will be happy flowering in a 9cm (3½in) pot.

Celosia plumosa Geisha Mixed: dwarf plants 20cm (8in) high with feathery, plume-like flowers in pink, red, and yellow shades, flowering in late summer; sow seed in late spring; pot on all celosias as quickly as possible to prevent them becoming pot-bound; grows best in a peat-based compost; may require as much as a 15cm (6in) pot.

Coleus blumei (syn. *Solenostemon scutellarioides*) cultivars: perennial shrubby plants usually grown as

*Gloxinias (*Sinningia speciosa*) can be purchased as tubers or grown from dust-like seed which is sown on the surface of peaty compost. F_1 hybrid mixes, such as Empress, will flower in mid-summer from a late winter sowing.*

annuals; popular for their brightly marked leaves; sow at any time but a late spring sowing will produce good sized plants in 13cm (5in) pots and good colour for the glasshouse from mid-summer into autumn; pinch out every two weeks to obtain a bushy plant and prevent flowering; named cultivars can be propagated successfully from cuttings taken in late summer.

Exacum affine: relative of the gentian; grows up to 25cm (10in) high; small, shiny leaves and many small, pale blue flowers with conspicuous yellow anthers; sow in early spring in a 13cm (5in) pot for summer to autumn flowering.

Impatiens (busy lizzie): more and more choice each year; single and double flowered cultivars of *I. walleriana* can be found in shades from white through to scarlet; the New Guinea *Impatiens* with attractive foliage and flowers was until recently obtainable only from cuttings but now can be raised from seed, New Guinea F_1 'Spectra'; sow the fine seed on a peaty seed compost from early spring; germinate in a warm propagator; prick out 2–3 weeks after sowing into trays and grow on at 15°C (60°F); will flower in 13–15cm (5–6in) pots from mid- to late summer onwards.

Petunia: popular bedding plants which suffer during wet summers when rain damages the flowers; if grown and raised as glasshouse pot plants or in hanging baskets, they will provide rewarding colour and scent; obtainable in a wide range of colours as well as doubles; sow in late spring and germinate in a warm propagator for flowering from mid-summer onwards in a 13cm (5in) pot; or pot three plants in a 20cm (8in) pot and train up canes to provide a pillar of flowers. F_1 Double Delight Mixed: double flowers in mixed shades from purple to pink and white; F_1 Picotee Mixed Colours: mixed colours with a white edge to the petals; F_1 'Super Magic Light Blue': light blue flowers.

Sinningia speciosa (gloxinia): belongs to the african violet family, Gesneriaceae; produces large, bell-shaped flowers above a rosette of large, deeply veined leaves; Mammoth Hybrids produce spotted and splashed flowers in a variety of colours; water from below as the leaves are easily marked by cold water; named cultivars can be obtained as corms for

starting into growth from mid-winter to early spring and flowering in a 13cm (5in) pot in summer. 'Gregor Mendel': large, double scarlet blooms edged with white is raised from seed sown in mid-winter to early spring on the surface of a peaty seed compost for summer flowering; will germinate at 20–25°C (68–77°F); prick out after a month into trays and grow at a minimum of 15°C (60°F); pot into 9cm (3½in) pots and finish off in a 13–15cm (5–6in) dwarf pot to give some protection to the brittle leaves.

Cacti and other succulents

Succulents are plants that have adapted to survive in harsh arid environments by storing water in their thick, fleshy leaves and stems. Cacti belong to a family of succulents, Cactaceae, that grow in the Americas. Many have large, swollen, water-storing stems, covered with groups of spines. In Africa, members of the spurge family, Euphorbiaceae, fill the same niche that cacti do in the Americas.

Both cacti and other succulents are extremely popular as hobby plants. There is a tremendous range of easy and more difficult plants to grow that are fairly small in size, so many different types can be grown in a small area. There are succulent plants which will thrive in all temperature ranges, but as a general rule of thumb, most cacti will grow happily in the cool glasshouse with a minimum winter temperature of 5°C (41°F), whereas many crassulas and kalanchoes are happier with a winter minimum of 10–15°C (50–60°F). Most succulent plants need good light and low humidity which makes them suitable for the sunny conservatory. Their growing season is from mid-spring to early autumn when there is sufficient light to allow growth. At this time plants will require most moisture, some needing watering two or three times a week, and feeding every two weeks, in hot, sunny weather. It is important, however, that succulents are allowed to dry out between waterings. They will soon rot if the compost remains too wet, and if you are in any doubt, do not water! In winter, growth will stop or be very slow, and the plants will need a cool, dry atmosphere and watering every four to six weeks at

***Crassula coccinea*
syn. *Rochea coccinea***
This small shrub, which can reach a height of 60cm (2ft), originates from South Africa. It is grown for its dramatic, carmine-red, tubular flowers that are produced in clusters on terminal growths in summer. After flowering, stems should be cut back to encourage the development of vigorous new shoots for flowering the following year. This also helps to keep plants vigorous and compact. Propagation is from seed or softwood and semi-ripe cuttings in spring.

the most. Plants kept too warm or wet in winter months will at best become drawn and misshapen and at worst rot off at the root.

Propagation and potting can take place from spring. I find that a soil-based compost with peat and grit added, provides an open, well-drained medium. Many succulents, such as *Kalanchoe* 'Tessa', can be propagated from stem cuttings, and *Epiphyllum* and *Schlumbergera* × *buckleyi* (christmas cactus) by removing and rooting one of the flat pads. A number of succulents with fleshy leaves can be propagated from leaf cuttings, with a new plant developing from the base of the leaf where it is in contact with the compost. Rosetted plants, like *Agave americana*, often produce offsets which are separated from the parent plant once they have produced their own roots. Cacti are raised easily from seed which germinates readily, but the plants take a long time to mature.

Recommended plants

Aeonium arboreum 'Atropurpureum': flat rosettes of dark purple; fleshy leaves; old specimens form curious, multi-stemmed plants.

Agave victoriae-reginae: medium-sized rosette 50cm (20in) in diameter, treasured for its silver streaks on the dark green leaves.

× *Aporophyllum* 'Wisewood': hanging basket plant with pendulous, succulent stems covered with spines; magenta and pink flowers in late winter to early spring.

Borzicactus aureispinus (syn. *Cleistocactus winteri*): suitable for large hanging baskets; thick, branching tubular stems covered with golden spines; red flowers in late spring.

Ceropegia woodii: trailing plant with small, attractively marked heart-shaped leaves; produces curious, tubular flowers in summer.

Crassula ovata (money plant): popular house plant; bushy with many fleshy, dark green leaves; clusters of flowers appear in spring.

Euphorbia milii (crown of thorns): narrow stems clothed with long spines and mid-green spatulate leaves; colourful bracts surround abundant small flowers in early spring to summer.

Hatiora gaertneri see *Schlumberga* × *buckleyi*.

Kalanchoe pumila: flat, grey leaves; attractive pink flowers in late winter to early spring.

Lithops (living stones): grown for the curious pairs of swollen leaves occurring at ground level which resemble pebbles; white or yellow daisy flowers in late summer or autumn.

Lobivia backebergii (syn. *Echinopsis backebergii*): clump-forming plant native to the Andes; some have lilac or red flowers in the late spring to mid-summer.

Mammillaria zeilmanniana: globular plant bearing single hooked spines surrounded by a ruff of fine spines; older plants will grow into clumps; pink-purple flowers in summer; mammillarias are one of the most popular small cacti.

Opuntia microdasys (bunny ears cactus): medium-sized plant with pad-like leaves covered with spots of silver or yellow spines.

Schlumbergera × *buckleyi* (christmas cactus) and *Hatiora gaertneri* (easter cactus): hybrids with a large colour range of flowers in mid-spring; originate from temperate and tropical forests; prefer moist fertile compost during the spring and summer; keep out of direct sunlight.

This mixed collection of small cacti, including Mammillaria, Rebutia *and* Lobivia, *thrives under cool glasshouse conditions where the minimum temperature is never lower than 5°C (41°F).*

Sedum morganianum: attractive hanging basket plant with trailing stems covered with short cylindrical leaves; star-shaped, rose-pink flowers in summer.

Pests and diseases

Cacti may suffer from mealy bugs, scale insects and tarsonemid mites (see pages 57 and 85). Corky scab, which is caused by a lack of light, too high a humidity or sun scorch, may also occur. The symptoms are rusty or corky spots which develop into sunken patches. It is controlled by correcting the levels of light and humidity.

Bulbous plants

There are many plants from all over the world that have underground storage organs to which the plant can retreat for protection during seasons with harsh weather, whether hot and dry as in a Mediterranean summer, or freezing cold as in an alpine winter. These storage organs can be grouped into four main categories – bulbs, corms, rhizomes and tubers. Bulbs are swollen leaf bases, a typical example being the daffodil bulb. Corms are swollen and compressed stems, for example cyclamen or crocus. Rhizomes are also swollen stems that frequently grow horizontally on the ground surface such as those found on irises. Dahlias and some ranunculus have tubers, which are swollen roots. However, in many catalogues such plants are all grouped together under the heading of bulbous plants, and, for the sake of simplicity, I will do the same.

It is important when buying bulbs to select only those that are sound and free from signs of pests and disease. Try to select the largest bulbs as they will have the biggest food reserves and the greatest potential flower power. As many natural habitats are being eroded due to pressure from human activity, it is essential that you buy bulbs rather than dig them up from the wild.

The majority of bulbs must be fed and watered from when they first emerge through the ground to when the foliage starts to die down in order to build up the underground storage organs and promote good flowers and growth the following season. When the leaves start to yellow, it indicates that

the plant is preparing for dormancy, and the compost should then be allowed to dry out. Pots of dormant bulbs, tubers or corms should be kept in a cool, dry position, such as under the glasshouse benching, until growth is resumed when they can be placed on the open bench. Bulbs grown in clay pots should have the pots sunk to the rim in a bed of sand to prevent the compost from over-drying which will cause the bulbs to dehydrate.

As a general rule the majority of bulbs should be potted into a well-drained, soil-based compost (such as John Innes No. 2) in plastic or clay pots, to a depth of two and a half times the height of the bulb. Exceptions to the rule are hippeastrums and nerines which should be potted so that the top third of the bulb is exposed above the compost. Large bulbs, such as hippeastrums, are potted singly into 15cm (6in) pots, while small bulbs are better potted in groups of five to ten bulbs to achieve a

*Glory lilies (*Gloriosa superba*) are an exotic addition to the temperate glasshouse. These climbers are usually bought as dormant tubers which will flower approximately three months after potting.*

satisfactory display. Most bulbs should be repotted each year into fresh compost, but a number of bulbous plants, for example nerines and crinums, flower better if kept pot-bound for a few years before repotting and then top-dressed with fresh compost each year before growth commences.

When the bulbs first come in to growth watering should be carried out with care, but once the foliage is fully grown, the compost will dry out more quickly and the plants will need regular waterings. Tender bulbs will require a minimum night temperature of 7–10°C (45–50°F), whereas tropical species will need a night minimum of 13–16°C (55–61°F).

Freesias

Freesia species originate from southern Africa. Modern cultivars are genetically improved (producing larger plants with larger flowers). Usually mixed colours only are available to the amateur.

Six corms should be planted 5cm (2in) deep into a 15cm (6in) pot from late summer to flower in winter, and mid-autumn for a spring flowering. The potted corms should be grown on in a cool glasshouse (4–7°C/40–45°F), gradually increasing watering as growth develops. Once seven leaves have formed per corm, the temperature should be increased to 10°C (50°F) and plants given regular liquid feeds – a high potash feed promoting flowering and preventing growth from becoming too soft. (Temperatures exceeding 20°C/68°F will induce vigorous leaf growth and a reduction in flowering.) Watering and feeding should continue for two months after flowering until the foliage starts to yellow. The compost should then be allowed to dry out. To initiate flowering inside the dormant corms, store them at a temperature of 30°C (86°F) for ten weeks of their dormant period, prior to replanting in late summer.

Freesias can also be grown from seed, sown between mid-spring and early summer, to flower from early autumn to spring. The seed has a hard coat and to aid germination you will need to rub the seed coat with a piece of sandpaper, then soak it in warm water for 24 hours. After sowing, cover the seed with approximately 6mm (¼in) of seed compost to allow the seed to germinate in the dark. Prick out the seedlings as soon as they can be handled easily, insert six or seven into a 15cm (6in) pot, and grow on at 12–15°C (54–60°F) until flowering. The growths can be supported by thin birch twigs to prevent them from toppling over.

Pests and diseases Freesias may suffer from aphids (see page 57), bulb rots and yellows. Bulb rots are caused by a variety of diseases which attack the corms during their dormant storage period. Affected corms should be discarded. Yellows first appears as yellow stripes between the leaf veins, followed by complete yellowing of the leaf and dieback. Corms sliced in half will be brown at their base. Affected plants should be destroyed. As a precautionary measure, corms should be dusted with a suitable fungicide prior to storing.

Glory lilies

Gloriosa superba is a climbing lily from tropical Africa which grows up to 1.5m (5ft) high and has reflexed red flowers with yellow margins. Plant the tubers from mid-winter to early summer, either two tubers per 17–20cm (7–8in) pot or one tuber per 14–16cm (5½–6½in) pot. Lay them horizontally and cover with 5cm (2in) of compost. Keep the pots at 20°C (68°F) to promote active growth and do not let the minimum night temperature fall below 17°C (63°F). Once in active growth they should be watered and fed regularly. The glasshouse should be damped down and ventilated during the summer to prevent arid, dry conditions, and the plants shaded from direct sunlight.

As the plant grows it will need the support of either a wigwam of bamboo canes or a circle of wire to which the plant should be regularly trained. Flowering will take place from the early spring, depending on the time of potting. After flowering, start to dry out the tubers and cut down the foliage once it has dried up. Tubers may be stored in plastic bags of dry sand at 10–15°C (50–60°F) until the next potting season.

Pests and diseases Glory lilies may suffer from aphids and whitefly (see page 57).

Zantedeschia aethiopica
The calla lily originates from South Africa and is named after Giovanni Zantedeschi, a 19th-century Italian botanist and physician. It is grown for its large, elegant, arum flowers, with yellow spadix and white, sail-like spathes which are produced under glass from early winter through to late spring. A moisture-loving plant, it may require watering every day, even in winter.

Hippeastrums (amaryllis)

Hippeastrum cultivars are popular winter-flowering plants, coming into bloom six to ten weeks after planting. Each flowering stem will carry three to four flowers and bulbs over 16cm (6½in) in diameter should produce two stems per bulb. They should be potted into pots twice the diameter of the bulb in a good soilless or soil-based compost (such as John Innes No. 2) from mid-autumn to early spring. After watering in, the pots should be placed where a temperature of 20–23°C (68–73°F) can be maintained, and after two weeks growth should start to take place, with flowering following after four to eight weeks. During flowering the temperature can be reduced to 15°C (60°F) to extend the life of the blooms. Water the bulbs and feed for no less than seven weeks after flowering, before drying and cutting off the leaves above the bulb. They should then be stored for two to three weeks at 23–25°C (73–77°F), and for a further eight to ten weeks at 13–17°C (55–63°F) before repotting and starting into growth.

Recommended cultivars 'Apple Blossom': pink with white centre; 'Ludwig Dazzler': white; 'Minerva': red with white centre; 'Red Lion': red; 'Rilona': salmon.

Pests and diseases Hippeastrums may suffer from aphids, mealy bugs and root mealy bugs (see page 57). They may also suffer from bulb scale mites and leaf scorch. Bulb scale mites live and feed in the neck of bulbs causing distortion, sickle-like curving of the leaves and saw-toothed notching along the leaf margins and flower stems. Flowers may also become distorted and stunted. Infected plants should be destroyed. Leaf scorch is a disease which appears as brown blotches at the leaf bases, on flower stalks and petals, which usually rot and become slimy. Infected parts should be cut out, and plants treated with a suitable fungicide.

Other suitable bulbs

Cyrtanthus parviflorus: narrow leaves and red tubular flowers borne in umbels in spring and summer; 15–20cm (6–8in).

Eucharis amazonica: paddle-shaped evergreen foliage; narcissus-like white flowers borne in umbels in summer; 30–60cm (1–2ft).

Haemanthus albiflos: wide strap-shaped leaves fringed with white hairs; white bottle brush flowers in late summer; 20cm (8in).

Lachenalia aloides: see page 114.

Lilium longiflorum (easter lily): large, fragrant, white trumpet flowers in early summer; 90cm (3ft).

Nerine sarniensis (guernsey lily): strap-shaped leaves; groups of 4–8 red or pink flowers borne in umbels in early autumn; 25–50cm (10–20in).

Sprekelia formosissima: strap-shaped leaves; crimson flowers in spring to early summer; 20–30cm (8–12in).

Zantedeschia aethiopica (calla lily): long stalked lanceolate leaves; elegant, white arum flowers from winter to summer; 1.5m (5ft).

Forcing hardy bulbs

It is possible to bring the beauty of a spring garden into the glasshouse or home in the depth of winter by forcing a wide variety of hardy bulbs. The bulbs are potted into pots or bowls from late summer to late autumn to give a period of flowering from early winter through to spring. Large bulbs, such as narcissus and hyacinth, have their necks protruding through the compost, whereas smaller bulbs like crocus and grape hyacinths (*Muscari*) should be planted 2.5cm (1in) deep. Selecting both early and late cultivars will further help to extend the flowering season.

The bulbs require a cool, moist period in which to break their dormancy and develop root systems before producing flowers and foliage. These conditions are best provided by placing the pots outside but protected from direct sunlight and covering them with a 10cm (4in) layer of sand. This keeps the compost moist and prevents rapid fluctuations in temperature. Prepared bulbs can be purchased, at an extra cost, which have been temperature-treated to break dormancy and promote earlier flowering. Remove the pots from the sand as soon as the foliage starts to emerge through the compost – for most bulbs this takes 10–12 weeks. Pots of bulbs can then be moved to a well-lit position and a temperature of 17°C (63°F) for forcing. Avoid forcing bulbous plants at higher temperatures as they will become drawn and top heavy before flowering. In order to stagger the flowering period of a particular cultivar, keep batches in cooler conditions, around 5°C (41°F) and introduce a batch each week to the warm conditions for forcing. In this way the flowering period can be spread out over six to eight weeks.

Bulbs may be potted into pots or bowls for display. Those planted in bowls without drainage holes must be watered carefully to avoid waterlogging. You can help keep the compost sweet by putting a layer of charcoal at the base of the bowl or potting with bulb fibre, which is a mixture of peat, charcoal and shell fragments.

Shorter bulbous plants, such as crocuses and miniature tulips, fortunately do not need staking to keep them upright, but many narcissus and hyacinth cultivars have a habit of flopping over when displayed in the warm home or conservatory and need supporting. Hyacinths can be staked once half the flowers have opened. Sharpen a thin split cane at one end, hold it alongside the flower stem and push the sharpened end through the bulb. Then cut the top of the cane to half the height of the flower spike and make a neat raffia tie just below the first flower. Although this sounds like a violent method of staking the hyacinth, it is the only way of getting the stake close to the flower stem without it looking too obvious and in fact causes no serious harm to the bulb. Pots of narcissus can be prevented from flopping by securing a loop of raffia around the foliage and flower stems, although this can look a little too formal. Another method is to push a split cane into the centre of the pot and with three or four loose ties secure groups of foliage and flowers to the central cane.

After flowering, pots of hardy bulbs can be planted outside for flowering in the garden the following year.

When buying bulbs for forcing, select only those that are firm and unscarred, with no sign of pests or disease. Plants from forced bulbs are generally pest- and disease-free, although young growths may suffer from aphids (see page 57).

Crocuses

Large flowered crocuses (*Crocus*), 10–15cm (4–6in) tall, should be planted in groups of 5–10 corms in half pots in early autumn for early to mid-winter flowering. Protect them from mice with wire netting. Recommended crocuses include: *C. × stellaris* 'Golden Yellow': yellow; *C. vernus* 'Pickwick': lilac with silvery feathery stripes; 'Queen of the Blues': blue; *C. vernus albiflorus* 'Snowstorm': white.

Hyacinths

Prepared hyacinth (*Hyacinthus*) bulbs should be potted in early autumn to flower by mid-winter. Unprepared bulbs should be potted from early to mid-autumn to flower in late winter to early spring. Flowers are 15–20cm (6–8in) tall. Buy larger bulbs for forcing and pot them directly into shallow bowls, or pot them into 9cm (3½in) pots and make up bowls once the flower colour is showing to obtain a better balance of height. Bowls of hyacinths are enhanced by covering the compost with a green moss. Recommended hyacinths include: *H. orientalis* 'Borah': many small spikes of blue flowers from one bulb; 'Delft Blue': blue; 'Jan Bos': red; 'L'Innocence': white; 'Pink Pearl': pink.

No mid-winter glasshouse display is complete without the sweet scent of hyacinths. Here, the intense blue spikes of Hyacinthus orientalis 'Blue Jacket' are complemented by the pink Primula obconica.

Narcissi

Unprepared bulbs are potted in early autumn for either a mid-winter flowering (early season) or a late winter to early spring flowering (mid-season). Prepared narcissus (*Narcissus*) bulbs are potted in mid- to late autumn for flowering in mid-winter. Recommended narcissi include: 'Grand Soleil d'Or' (prepared bulb): bunch flowered with beautifully scented yellow flowers; not frost-hardy and unsuitable for planting outdoors except in mild areas; 38cm (15in); 'Ice Follies': white flowers with flat crown and pale yellow frills; 45cm (1½ft); mid-season; 'Paper White' (prepared bulb): similar to 'Grand Soleil d'Or' but with smaller white flowers; can flower 6 weeks from potting.

Tulips

Tulips (*Tulipa*) should be potted from early to mid-autumn and brought into the glasshouse for forcing from mid- to late winter. Flowering will take place from late winter to mid-spring. Recommended tulips include: 'Apricot Beauty': salmon-pink; 40cm (16in); *T. kaufmanniana*: creamy white centre with carmine red markings; 15cm (6in); 'Mr van der Hoef': golden yellow; 30cm (12in); 'Oranje Nassau': fiery red; 30cm (12in); 'Red Riding Hood': purple-brown markings on leaves; scarlet flowers; 20cm (8in); *T. tarda*: 2–3 flowers on each stem; yellow with white tips; 15cm (6in).

Perennial climbers

Climbers serve as the backcloth drapes for the display glasshouse and can be used effectively in both the landscaped and benched glasshouse to soften their rigid structure and provide a vertical backdrop against which other plants can be displayed (see also page 83).

Support for these plants should be erected before planting and must be capable of taking the full weight of the established climber. Self-clinging climbers, such as ivies, will adhere to vertical surfaces with adventitious roots growing from the stems. Plants with twining stems, such as *Jasminum polyanthum*, may be trained as small pot plants to a wire loop. A more established plant in the glass-

The vigorous growth of bougainvilleas, such as B. 'Poulton's Special' shown here trained up a supporting pillar, provides a dramatic display of vivid pink bracts throughout the summer.

house border or in a 20–25cm (8–10in) pot, will make an effective display if a number of vertical wires are arranged in a fan formation, allowing the vigorous shoots to spread out. Passion flowers (*Passiflora*) have tendrils which they use to attach themselves to their supports of wires or trelliswork. I have found that the best method of displaying passion flowers is to train them along horizontal wires, stretched between the eaves of the glasshouse. Main shoots run along the wires producing a good crop of flowers, but the best display comes from the lateral shoots which cascade down forming a curtain of foliage and flowers.

Rambling climbers, like bougainvilleas, cling to their supports with their numerous spines but when grown in the glasshouse they need to be regularly tied in to a strong support such as a trellis, wires or pergola. Many free-standing shrubby plants can be grown and trained to vertical supports and with careful training and pruning will show off their flowers to good effect. A good example of a shrubby plant is the lax growing *Abutilon megapotamicum*, whose thin shoots can be trained up wires or trellis and then allowed to hang down, creating a cascade of flowers and foliage.

The ideal glasshouse for growing and displaying many climbers is a lean-to, where the back wall can support wires or trelliswork. Where walls are not available wires can be fixed to the glasshouse with vine eyes (see page 75), either on the side wall or stretched between the eaves, placing them so that the growing climber will cast little shade on other glasshouse plants. It is much easier to train climbers if wires are straight and taut. Straining bolts or barrel tensioners will take up any slack in the wire.

I often hear complaints from gardeners saying that their climbers seldom flower. After some discussion it usually transpires that the gardener has been overwhelmed by summer growth and, by way of revenge, has brought the climbers into line with a hard pruning, unknowingly removing growth that would produce flowers the following spring. This goes to show how important it is to understand the growing and flowering cycle of a climber before you embark on any pruning.

Most climbers can be divided into two categories – those that flower on the current season's growth, usually in the summer and autumn; and those that flower on the previous year's growth, usually in the winter and spring. Plants belonging to the first category are best pruned in late winter, giving them enough time to produce sufficient growth to flower later in the year. Good examples are *Plumbago auriculata* and *Ipomoea acuminata*. Such climbers can be cut back to buds in old wood to encourage the development of vigorous new shoots. However, where there has been excessive growth, this will cast too much shade on the other glasshouse plants if left over winter. In such cases I prefer to prune out half the shoots in the autumn, leaving the rest for the main prune in late winter. Climbers flowering in winter and spring usually do so on growth formed the previous summer. Popular examples are *Acacia baileyana* and *Clianthus puniceus* which are best pruned immediately after flowering.

Pruning should only be carried out with a sharp knife or secateurs – blunt tools will make tearing cuts which may result in die-back and diseased shoots. When pruning always cut back to just above a bud; do not leave snags which will die back and encourage infection as well as look unsightly. First remove any dead, diseased or dying growth, then cut out any overcrowded or crossing shoots. Finally, select and tie in growth both for flower and extension growth. Shoots should be tied in with soft string, making sure that soft, young growths are not tied too tightly to prevent the restriction of future growth (girdling). It is important to check all the ties regularly and retie any that have become too tight. Plants with twining shoots or tendrils will generally support themselves with little training, but rambling climbers or trained shrubs should have their shoots tied in to a framework at regular intervals when in active growth. If left too long, the shoots will become unmanageable. Where a plant has settled down and regularly produces good flowers, pruning can be restricted to keeping the plant within bounds and removing any dead wood or old flowered shoots. More severe pruning will only be necessary every few years to rejuvenate a tired plant.

For the small glasshouse owner who wishes to grow a number of plants in a small space, there are many climbers that grow and flower very well in containers. Bougainvilleas are a fine example. Less vigorous cultivars such as *B.* × *buttiana* 'Mrs Butt' with rose-crimson papery bracts, the semi-double *B. glabra* 'Snow White' or any of the variegated forms like *B.* 'Raspberry Ice', will flourish in 20–30cm (8–12in) pots. During the winter bougainvilleas should be kept only slightly moist and they will withstand cool glasshouse conditions. Extensive periods at temperatures below 4°C (40°F) will cause them to drop their leaves but this will not matter as long as the plants are kept dry. In late winter they should be pruned hard into a sparse framework one or two buds from the previous year's growth, and then top-dressed with fresh compost (such as John Innes No. 2). To force the plants into growth requires warm conditions of about 22°C (72°F) and regular weekly feeds with a high nitrogen fertilizer. Pinch the shoots to encourage a well-branched plant and while they are still supple train them up a fan or around a wigwam of bamboo canes. The papery bract flowers will appear at the end of each shoot from mid-summer onwards. This can be advanced by reducing nitrogen and using a higher potash feed which hardens up the growths. Once the bracts have faded the shoots can be shortened to encourage fresh growth and flowers.

Passion flowers (*Passiflora*) are good pot subjects if grown in 23cm (9in) pots and trained up a wigwam of canes. Some of the more vigorous species, such as *P. edulis*, will need regular trimming to prevent them from overwhelming the glasshouse. Temperate and tropical species of *Passiflora*, such as *P. mollissima* and *P.* × *caponii* 'John Innes', are particularly successful pot plants. A word of warning, though – they are apt to suffer from neck rot if they get too cold in the winter, so it is always a good idea to root a few cuttings in the summer as an insurance policy in case a prize plant succumbs in the winter.

Below I have listed other perennial climbers suited to glasshouse cultivation. I have not given measurements for any of the plants as these can vary considerably depending on how they are grown.

Rhodochiton atrosanguineum

The purple bell vine is a perennial climbing plant from Mexico. The botanical name describes the unusual flower – rhodon *means rose, and* chiton *refers to the large calyx (group of sepals) which resembles a cloak. The flower consists of a conspicuous, red, bell-shaped calyx from which a narrow, maroon, tubular flower hangs.*

Abutilon: see page 110.

Acacia (wattle): see page 110.

Allamanda cathartica (golden trumpet): see page 122.

Aristolochia elegans (dutchman's pipe): manageable climber with twining stems and heart-shaped leaves; elegant brown-marked flowers in spring and summer; propagate from seed or cuttings in spring.

Bignonia capreolata (cross vine): vigorous climber with pairs of lanceolate leaves; climbs with tendrils; orange-red tubular flared flowers borne on previous year's growth in late spring; propagate from seed or cuttings in spring.

Bougainvillea: many cultivars; see page 111.

Buddleja asiatica: medium-sized shrub which can be trained against a trellis; downy lanceolate leaves and drooping panicles of small, white, fragrant flowers from late winter to spring; propagate from seed or cuttings in spring.

Cestrum aurantiacum: see page 116.

Chorizema ilicifolium: small, wiry shrub; lanceolate leaves suitable for trailing through other trellis plants; red and orange pea-shaped flowers in spring and summer; propagate from seed in spring or cuttings in late summer.

Clerodendrum thomsoniae (bleeding heart vine): see page 122.

Clianthus puniceus (lobster claw): see page 113.

Cytisus canariensis (syn. *Genista canariensis*): see page 113.

Fuchsia fulgens: medium-sized shrub which can be trained against trellis to show off the cascading shoots with clusters of scarlet, tubular flowers tipped with green borne in summer; propagate from seed or cuttings in spring.

Hoya carnosa (wax plant): vigorous, twining climber with thick, fleshy, glossy leaves; umbels of white flowers, which are fragrant at night, borne from late spring to autumn; popular pot plant; propagate from seed or cuttings in spring.

Jasminum (jasmine): see page 113.

Lapageria rosea (chilean bell flower): see page 114.

Plumbago auriculata (syn. *P. capensis*): see page 114.

Tetrastigma voinierianum (chestnut vine): vigorous foliage climber with attractive divided leaves covered with a brown felt when young; propagate from seed or tip cuttings in spring.

Climbers grown as annuals from seed

As well as permanent climbers, there are many that can be raised annually from seed and used to fill in the gaps in a trellis, grown up canes, or on twiggy growths in pots for an unusual bench display. Sow seed in pots or trays in mid-spring and germinate at 15–20°C (60–68°F). Once germination is complete the seedlings should be pricked out singly into 8cm (3in) pots in a soil-based compost (such as John Innes No. 2) or alternative soilless compost. Place a short, split cane next to the seedling to support the developing twining shoots. Once the shoots have reached the top of the cane, the plant is ready to plant out, either to grow up existing trellis and wires, or up to six plants may be planted in a 30cm (12in) pot and provided with canes or twiggy growth up which to climb. If properly hardened off, many of these annually sown climbers can be planted outside as soon as all risk of frost has passed. In the summer, wires or trellis erected on the outside of the glasshouse will allow these annual climbers to grow upwards and provide an attractive living shading for the glasshouse. If their growth casts too much shade, they can be thinned out lightly. The climbers will be killed off by the first frosts and can be removed to allow more light into the glasshouse for the autumn.

It is possible to grow your own sponges under glass in the summer. The loofah sponge, *Luffa cylindrica*, is an annual climber that is related to the cucumber and can be cultivated in the same way. It can reach 4m (13ft) in height and has large leaves and twining tendrils. The sponges are produced by removing the skin of a ripe fruit and washing the flesh and seeds from the rubbery skeleton of the fruit, which is allowed to dry out. It is then ready to use.

The following is a list of climbers – perennials and annuals – that can be raised each year in the glasshouse, propagated from seed sown in spring.
Cobaea scandens (cathedral bell, cup and saucer vine): vigorous climber growing up to 5m (16ft) in one year; pinnate leaves with ovate leaflets terminating

in a tendril; pale green, ageing to purple, bell-shaped flowers in summer and early autumn.
Eccremocarpus scaber (chilean glory flower): vigorous climber growing up to 5m (16ft) in one year; bipinnate leaves terminating in tendrils; orange, yellow or red tubular flowers in summer to autumn.
Ipomoea lobata: twining climber growing up to 3m (10ft); five-lobed leaves; clusters of tubular, crimson, ageing to yellow, flowers in summer.
Ipomoea quamoclit (cypress vine): annual climber growing up to 5m (16ft); fine, fern-like, pinnate leaves; scarlet, tubular flowers in summer.
Thunbergia alata (black-eyed susan): climber with twining stems growing up to 3m (10ft); pale yellow to orange flowers with a dark brown centre borne in summer; triangular leaves.
Tropaeolum majus (nasturtium): annual climber growing up to 3m (10ft); almost round leaves; large red, orange or yellow, spurred flowers produced from summer to autumn; edible flowers, leaves and seeds.
Tropaeolum peregrinum (canary creeper): annual climber growing up to 4m (13ft); leaf made up of five to seven ovate lobes; long leaf stems provide anchorage; fringed yellow flowers in summer.

The chilean glory flower (Eccremocarpus scaber) is a perennial climber which will not withstand serious frosts outdoors. It is best raised from seed saved each year, and flowers from mid-summer until the first frosts of autumn.

THROUGH THE SEASONS

I remember as a child visiting an uncle in mid-Wales for a late spring holiday and being astonished to see that the daffodils in his garden were still in full bloom, whereas ours at home in London had completed their flowering three weeks earlier. As climatic conditions vary so much from region to region, I have avoided giving precise dates when various horticultural tasks should be carried out in the glasshouse and given instead the season, which I believe is far more helpful.

Although there may still be snow on the ground outside in late winter and early spring, the glasshouse can be full of colour, with pots of flowering bulbs and autumn-sown annuals, such as Schizanthus 'Hit Parade', here complemented by the graceful flowers of Zantedeschia aethiopica.

Spring

It is easy to be lulled into a false sense of security after a few sunny days in spring. You may think that summer has come and start hardening plants off, only to find that the glasshouse is covered with snow the next day. Sunny days and cool nights will bring about great fluctuations in glasshouse temperatures, causing plants to dry out suddenly. It is a good idea to anticipate the weather even if you are going away for just the day so that plants can be well watered in the early morning and adequate ventilation provided during the day.

This is the most important time of the year in the glasshouse – sowing, pricking out and potting plants if done at the correct times will bear fruition later in the year. Because of the increasing light and rising temperatures, plants propagated in spring generally root or germinate quickly and, having a long period of ideal conditions in which to grow, will make the most healthy plants.

Once the average daily temperature rises above 6°C (43°F), garden plants will come into growth and a careful eye must be kept on those intended for propagation so that softwood cuttings can be taken once the shoots are long enough. As temperatures rise, pests become an increasing problem and should be controlled as soon as they are noticed. You can start to introduce biological controls from early spring, and use yellow sticky traps to attract flying insects and as indicators to pest populations, provided you change them regularly.

Early spring

Water and ventilate with great care as plants not used to bright sunshine may wilt while remaining moist at the roots. Spraying over the foliage and shading will help to reduce water loss from the leaves. Apply shading paint to the exterior of the glasshouse.

The start of spring is heralded by the flowering of summer- and autumn-sown annuals.

Cold glasshouse and frame: Plant out lettuce sown in mid-winter either directly into the glasshouse border, frame, or outside in the garden under a cloche, or in old tomato bags from the previous summer. Up to 10 lettuces can be raised in one bag. Remember to flush the bags through with clean water before planting.
Heated glasshouse: Remember to shade propagation environments such as closed cases and polythene tents from direct sunlight to prevent temperatures rising too quickly and 'cooking' sensitive plants. Force dahlia tubers by boxing them up in moist peat and providing a minimum temperature of 15°C (60°F) so that softwood cuttings can be taken from the developing shoots. Sow seeds of F_1 cyclamen for winter flowering and schizanthus and salpiglossis for summer flowering in the glasshouse. Sow tomatoes, cucumbers and melons. Plant out early tomatoes, such as 'Dombello' and F_1 'Shirley', which were sown in mid-winter to crop in early summer.

Mid-spring

Wind and sudden showers can be a problem at this time and careful ventilation will be needed as cold air and drips through the ventilators will damage young plants. The most effective solution is to close the ventilators on the windward side and on the leeward side have them open below horizontal so that rain will run off. Warm sunny days will promote rapid growth in all plants, so make sure that you water adequately in the morning to last the plants through the day. Damping down gravel benches and the glasshouse paths will help to maintain a buoyant atmosphere and reduce drying. Regularly knock plants out of their pots to check their root systems. Plants can quickly become pot-bound and starved of nutrients if they are not potted on in time.

Cold glasshouse and frame: Harden off half-hardy plants to make more room in the heated glasshouse for bedding plants and vegetables, such as cucumbers and tomatoes.
Heated glasshouse: Pot on bedding and conservatory plants to ensure rapid development. Improved outside temperatures and light will have brought many shrubs and herbaceous plants into growth, so keep an eye on any plants, such as lilac (*Syringa*) and buddleja, that can be propagated from softwood cuttings inserted in a heated frame or glasshouse propagator. Sow seed of *Kalanchoe blossfeldiana* for late winter flowering as well as tobacco plants such as *Nicotiana sylvestris* and *N. rustica* for planting out in the garden once the frosts are over in early summer. Continue to sow pots of herbs such as basil and dill to cut for the kitchen. Start to shade the glasshouse as the light intensity can be strong enough to scorch some plants; apply shading to the sunny side of the glasshouse first. Prune winter and spring flowering shrubs as soon as the flowers have faded and train in any new growth on shrubby

climbers. Carefully tie in shoots to the training wires on vines grown under glass and pinch out flowering growths two leaves beyond each flower cluster.

Late spring

Cold glasshouse and frame: Harden off bedding plants in frames so that they will be ready for planting out in early summer. Plant up hanging baskets and harden off in a cold frame or cold glasshouse – the baskets are best supported on a pot to keep them upright and off the ground.

Heated glasshouse: Take cuttings of kalanchoes such as the trailing *Kalanchoe* 'Tessa' and *K. manginii*. Sow coleus, petunias, celosias, busy lizzies (*Impatiens*) and calendulas for growing in pots in the glasshouse, and annual climbers, such as *Ipomoea tricolor* 'Heavenly Blue' or black-eyed susan (*Thunbergia alata* 'Susie') for planting outside. Plant aubergines, sweet peppers, cucumbers and melons in the glasshouse border, pots or growing bags, making sure that you water well before and after planting.

Summer

The highest light intensities occur in early summer and under these conditions plants dry out rapidly and should be checked for watering at least three times a day. Special attention should be paid to pot-bound plants and those in small pots or growing bags, which tend to dry out quickly. Rapidly growing plants receiving a lot of water will need increased feeding – up to twice a week to maintain their growth rate without risking nutrient deficiencies. Increase shading, provide good ventilation and regularly damp down the glasshouse floors to maintain a humid, buoyant atmosphere. Damping down will also encourage the formation of algae which should be removed with a motorized pressure

Coleus blumei *hybrids provide a stunning range of foliage colour in the summer.*

washer, or a firm broom, soapy water and lots of elbow grease. Algaecides prevent the formation of algae and need to be applied frequently to the glasshouse floor during the summer months as their effect is short-lived due to the constant damping down.

The constant warm conditions will encourage the rapid increase of pests. Plants should be checked at regular intervals and treated with an appropriate pesticide or regular introductions of biological controls, as soon as any pests are spotted.

Early summer

Cold glasshouse and frame: In early to midsummer softwood and semi-ripe cuttings of herbaceous plants and shrubs can be taken and inserted directly into a shaded cold frame. Sow large-flowered foxgloves (*Digitalis*), such as *D. purpurea* Excelsior Hybrids, for growing in pots in the cold glasshouse. The vine border should be fed to help fruit development, and the

swelling bunches of fruit thinned to prevent them from overcrowding and the fruit from splitting.

Heated glasshouse: Make sure that cucumbers are harvested as soon as they are mature to ensure a continuous supply. Tomato plants must be watered sufficiently to prevent drying out. Irregular watering will result in blossom end rot and the fruit splitting. Spray over the plants at midday to aid fruit setting. If growth loses vigour, use feeds with an increased nitrogen ratio.

Mid-summer

Mid-summer is the best time to carry out any major structural maintenance or alterations to the glasshouse. It is warm enough outside for most plants to survive without protection as long as they are out of direct sunlight.

Cold glasshouse and frame: Harvest tomatoes and pinch out the central growing point on cordon-trained plants two leaves after the fifth flower truss. Bush tomatoes in frames should be mulched with straw to keep the fruit off the soil. Check cuttings inserted the previous month. Remove fallen or diseased leaves.

Heated glasshouse: Sow cineraria and calceolaria cultivars for an early spring flowering. For a late winter to spring display, sow primulas such as *Primula acaulis* on the surface of a soilless compost, at a temperature of 15–18°C (60–65°F). Avoid higher temperatures which will inhibit seedling development. Pick over faded flowers of summer flowering plants, removing fading blooms and seed heads to help extend the flowering season.

Late summer

Cold glasshouse and frame: Harden off rooted cuttings inserted in the frame in early summer by increasing ventilation before potting. With the frame cleared of plants, semi-ripe cuttings of evergreen shrubs can be inserted so that they root before the winter. Prick out annuals sown the previous month into 8–9cm (3–3½in) pots and place in a well-ventilated frame. Sow seed of hardy cyclamen and primulas. Pot up strawberries for forcing in the cold glasshouse in winter.

Heated glasshouse: Sow schizanthus, clarkias and echiums. Take cuttings of pelargoniums, fuchsias and begonias and other half-hardy plants from the garden that can be rooted in a heated frame or glasshouse propagator. If away on holiday, help 'plant sitters' by setting up an automatic watering system for the period you are away. Watering and damping down three times a day is a lot to ask of someone.

Autumn

Autumn is the transition period between summer and winter, and summer, winter and intermediate conditions can be experienced throughout the season. In early autumn, the days can be dry and sunny but the nights soon start to get cold and some heating may be required to keep out frosts. As autumn progresses the days become shorter, cooler and damper, with increasing spells of frost and fog by late autumn. It is vital to keep an eye on weather forecasts, not only for frost warnings, but also for high winds and gales which can cause considerable damage to frames and glasshouses if they are not closed in advance.

Early autumn

Early autumn is the best time to give the glasshouse interior a good tidy and clean before it is filled with plants needing protection from the cold. Scrub down the glass with soapy water to remove all traces of shading paint and any algae or dirt that has built up over the spring and summer period. With small glasshouses remove all the plants and stand them outside

Spray chrysanthemums are brought into the glasshouse in early autumn for protection.

during the cleaning – it makes access easier and prevents any possible damage. Remove moss growing between the glass and glazing bars as drips from the moss can splash seed pots and make plants too damp. Use a sharpened cane or, where the moss is held fast, a motorized pressure washer. Once the inside of the glasshouse is clean, insulation materials such as bubble polythene can be installed to reduce winter heating costs. Before the autumn rains it is advisable to check that the gutters are clear and do not become clogged with fallen leaves. Reduced sunlight means that glasshouse shading can be removed.

Cold glasshouse and frame: Sow lettuce for cutting in early spring. Prick out late summer-sown annuals and continue to pot on those sown in mid-summer. Remove the frame lights over annuals during clear days, cover but leave good ventilation in wet weather, and close the frame and cover with insulation for protection on

frosty nights. Buy spring flowering bulbs and store *Narcissus* 'Paper White' in a refrigerator for potting in late autumn. Pot up other bulbs and store in a cool, moist position until growth is seen above the soil.

Heated glasshouse: Protect glasshouse fruit from vermin by putting down traps for rodents and covering the ventilators with netting to keep birds out. Pot on rooted cuttings of pelargoniums, begonias and fuchsias so that they can become established in 9cm (3½in) pots before winter. Pot up half-hardy plants such as cannas and stock plants of fuchsias and pelargoniums from the garden, so that they can be over-wintered in a frost-free position. Sow lettuce for cutting in early winter.

Mid-autumn

Cold glasshouse and frame: Sow lettuce in a cold glasshouse for harvesting in mid-spring. Harvest the last of the tomatoes. Ripen fruit that is still green in a drawer or can with an apple, or make green tomato chutney. Continue to pot on annuals and make sure they are well spaced out in the frame so that they receive the maximum amount of light. Close frames and cover at night to protect from frost.

Heated glasshouse: As the sun loses its strength and humidity rises, plants grow more slowly and require less water. Reduce damping down to the mornings of sunny days as humidities are now generally too high. Complete any propagation as plants take longer to root as the quality of light deteriorates. Sow open pollinated cyclamen hybrids after soaking the seed in tepid water for 24 hours.

Late autumn

Cold glasshouse and frame: Sow lettuce for harvesting in late spring. Sow seeds of herbaceous plants and shrubs in pots and place in a cold frame to break their dormancy. Pot up *Narcissus* 'Paper White' and place with the other pots of bulbs. Prepared hyacinths may start growing and should be placed in a well-lit cold frame before forcing.

Heated glasshouse: Sow lettuce for harvesting in early spring. Once serious frosts threaten, remove annuals from the cold frame and bring into the glasshouse and grow in a well-ventilated and lit position. Lift crowns of seakale, rhubarb and chicory from the vegetable garden for forcing in the dark under the glasshouse bench. Prune vines after the leaves have dropped, cutting back the year's growth to one or two buds.

Winter

It is important to make sure that all frost-tender plants are kept safe in the heated glasshouse, which in the worst winter conditions will need heating both day and night. Make the most of any mild, sunny winter days to ventilate the glasshouse and remove the stagnant, humid air. Even plants in the warm tropical glasshouse will stop growing in the depth of winter due to lack of light and for this reason watering should be kept to a minimum and damping down stopped until late winter when the light starts to increase in quality. Snow settling on the glasshouse should be removed with a long handled brush as its weight can damage the glasshouse and cut out light. Avoid propagating any plants in the early and mid-winter period as light levels are too low to permit sufficient growth. Pest problems are usually at their minimum in the winter as temperatures are not high enough for them to breed quickly. Use this to your advantage by cleaning up any infested plants by spraying and fumigating the glasshouse. Biological controls are only effective in the warmest glasshouses in winter and generally are best introduced once temperatures start to increase from late winter onwards. Make sure all exposed water pipes and taps are

Catch up on glasshouse tasks in winter when outside cultivation is impossible.

lagged or drained off to prevent them from bursting in freezing conditions.

Early winter

Cold glasshouse and frame: Check plants and remove any dead or diseased foliage. Keep a look-out for rodents which will burrow in pots for bulbs and large seeds. Protect plants in the frame by placing a wire covering over the frame and set baited traps.

Heated glasshouse: Force bulbs in a frost-free glasshouse for flowering mid- to late winter, remembering to stake bulbs before they start to flop over. Check all glasshouse plants for grey mould and remove any dead or diseased leaves. Peel loose bark off the dormant vines (be careful around the buds) to expose over-wintering pests to winter pesticide treatment. Order catalogues from seed merchants and nurseries so you can plan the glasshouse campaign for the next growing season in the warmth and comfort of your home.

Mid-winter

Cold glasshouse and frame: See under Early winter.

Heated glasshouse: Continue to force chicory, seakale and rhubarb under the glasshouse bench to provide delicious early crops. Lift and pot runners of mint and clumps of chives to force in the frost-free glasshouse for early spring. Plant out strawberries in the open ground and cover with a cloche or low polythene tunnel. Alternatively, force the strawberries in pots in a frost-free glasshouse for harvesting in mid- to late spring. Pot up hippeastrum bulbs and start into growth in the warmth. Growth should start to take place after two weeks, with flowers often appearing before the leaves. Sow seeds of *Begonia semperflorens* and F_1 pelargoniums.

Late winter

Sudden spells of sunny weather can cause glasshouse temperatures to rise dramatically. On such days ventilate from mid-morning to prevent too much cold air entering the glasshouse.

Cold glasshouse and frame: Plant lettuce sown the previous month in a cold frame or glasshouse and harvest in mid- to late spring.

Heated glasshouse: Sow aubergines and peppers from now until early spring. Seed of conservatory plants such as abutilons and cordylines may be sown as this gives them a long season to grow and develop before the following winter. Take chrysanthemum cuttings and place in a cold frame or under mist to root. Start the vine into growth towards the middle of the month by increasing the temperature to 15°C (60°F) and irrigate the vine border thoroughly. Damp down the floors and vine rods three times each day to encourage the even breaking of buds along the rod. Bring other fruit in pots, such as figs, peaches and nectarines, into growth.

KEY PLANTS

This selection of plants is a personal choice of those that offer year-round interest and challenge in the glasshouse. Included is a range of rewarding plants from both temperate and tropical regions which can be grown to create an exotic glasshouse garden, as well as those plants that spend only a part of their lives under glass, whether for propagation or for winter protection.

The heady fragrance of Gardenia jasminoides 'Fortuniana', fashionable in the Edwardian glasshouse, will fill even the largest glasshouse during the main flowering period of summer and autumn. Gardenias thrive in the warm temperate glasshouse in the semi-shade, but dislike cold draughts which cause them to drop their unopened flower buds.

Large groups of popular glasshouse plants, such as begonias, as well as fruit and vegetables, are not to be found in this checklist as I have discussed them in depth in the chapters on the productive glasshouse (see page 59) and the display glasshouse (see page 81). Specialist glasshouse plants, such as orchids, do not feature either as so many have specialist cultural requirements and are difficult to grow with a mixed collection of plants.

In the summary to each entry I have given the maximum expected height and spread for each group of plants, although this figure can be reduced considerably by container growing to restrict the roots, and by careful pruning. The spread is not given for climbers as this will depend on the size of support on which the climber is growing.

I have grouped plants according to the minimum temperature range they need to flourish: frost-free 4–10°C (40–50°F); temperate 10–15°C (50–60°F); and tropical 15–20°C (60–68°F).

Frost-free glasshouse

Abutilon

These South American shrubs have maple-like leaves and produce colourful, bell-shaped flowers over a long season. A number of cultivars have colourful yellow or cream variegated foliage. If kept relatively dry during the winter, many will survive periods of frost. Although these plants are propagated easily from softwood or semi-ripe cuttings at any time of year, I prefer to take cuttings in late summer and over-winter young plants. Plants can be grown in pots for glasshouse display or bedded out in early summer after the last frost. With a free root-run, vigorous cultivars can grow up to 2m (6½ft) in one season.

Cultivars include: 'Boule de Neige', with pure white flowers and mid-green foliage; 'Canary Bird', with large, yellow, cupped flowers; 'Kentish Belle': large orange-yellow flowers; 'Nabob', with deep crimson bells; 'Souvenir de Bonn', with orange-yellow flowers with deep pink veins and dark green, maple-like leaves margined with creamy yellow. *A. × hybridum* 'Savitzii' is a less vigorous plant suitable for pots, with white splashed foliage and orange-yellow flowers. *A. megapotamicum* is a lax shrub with wiry shoots, long and narrow heart-shaped leaves, and pendulous flowers with bright red sepals and yellow petals. *A. megapotamicum* 'Variegatum', one of the more frost-hardy abutilons, has attractive mottled leaves and is worth raising for its foliage alone. It is best grown as a wall shrub supported by wires or trellis, and young specimens can be grown in hanging baskets.

A. × milleri is similar in habit to *A. megapotamicum*, but has larger, yellow veined flowers. *A. pictum* (syn. *A. striatum*) has maple-like leaves and pendulous red flowers with attractive reticulate orange veins. Its cultivar 'Thompsonii' has striking mottled foliage. *A. × suntense* is a deciduous, frost-hardy shrub with vine-shaped leaves, growing up to 2.5m (8ft), and available in colours from white through to deep purple.
Size H: 2–5m/6½–16ft; S: 2–3m/6½–10ft. **Season of interest** All year for coloured foliage plants; spring, summer and autumn for flowers.
Propagation Seed in spring for species; softwood and semi-ripe cuttings throughout the year for species and named cultivars.

Acacia
(Wattle)

These shrubs and small trees are grown for their evergreen foliage and balls of yellow 'mimosa' flowers borne in late winter and spring. They are best grown in full sun, and in pots which helps to restrict the growth of the more vigorous species and encourages them to flower while young. Prune all species directly after flowering. Some species will take a few degrees of frost and are suitable for the cold glasshouse or protected garden border in mild climates. Do not allow plants to become too dry in late summer as this can affect the formation of flower buds.

A. armata (kangaroo thorn) is a compact species with winged, bristly, dark green shoots and rich yellow flowers in spring. *A. baileyana* (cootamunda wattle) is a small pendulous tree with double pinnate, blue-grey leaves, and rich yellow flowers in late winter. It is hardy in mild climates. *A. dealbata* (mimosa) is sold by florists in spring for its attractive grey-green foliage and fluffy, scented, yellow flowers. It is hardy in mild climates if grown against a warm wall. The graceful, pendulous *A. longifolia* has long, narrow leaves and cylindrical clusters of pale yellow flowers in early spring, while the bushy shrub, *A. podalyriifolia*, has attractive, silvery-blue, winged foliage, and rich yellow flowers in spring.
Size H: 3–15m/10–49ft; S: 2–8m/6½–26ft). **Season of interest** Late winter to spring. **Propagation** Seed in early spring; semi-ripe heel cuttings in early summer.

Alyogyne huegelii
'Santa Cruz'

This relative of the hibiscus is grown for its wonderful soft blue flowers measuring up to 8cm (3in) across, and deep green, lobed leaves. It will grow rapidly and make a large shrub but, if thinned in autumn and cut back to a low framework of branches in late winter, it will stay easily within its bounds. As with all members of the mallow (Malvaceae) family, 'Santa Cruz' is beloved of whitefly!
Size H: to 3m/10ft; S: to 2m/6½ft. **Season of interest** Spring and summer. **Propagation** Softwood and semi-ripe cuttings in spring and summer.

Asparagus

Asparagus are grown for their ferny, spiny or awl-shaped foliage which consists of phylloclades (to be botanically correct). These are modified stems resembling leaves, although they are not true leaves. Many species have small, star-shaped flowers which are followed by pea-sized berries. They make good pot plants, but are best re-propagated every few years from seed as the pots eventually become overcrowded and severely potbound by the thick fleshy roots.

A. densiflorus from South Africa has long, arching stems covered with fine, branched phylloclades and red fruit. 'Meyeri' makes a medium-sized plant and looks strangely like a bunch of drooping cats' tails! 'Sprengeri' makes a good edging or background plant and produces many stems covered with groups of three to four

phylloclades, producing a finer texture than 'Meyeri'. *A. setaceus* (asparagus fern) is a climbing species reaching up to 3m (10ft). It is grown for its fine, frond-like foliage borne at regular intervals along the stems. 'Compacta', as its name suggests, is more compact and better suited to the small glasshouse and pot growing.
Size H: 60cm–3m/2–10ft; S: 120cm–2m/4–6½ft. **Season of interest** All year. **Propagation** Seed and division in spring.

Aztec lily see *Sprekelia formosissima*

Bitter orange see under *Citrus*

Bougainvillea

These vigorous climbing plants with spiny stems are grown for their stunning papery bracts (modified leaves), available in a great variety of colours. Plants should be lightly pruned after flowering in summer and then hard pruned in late winter (see page 100). Plants may be trained up trellises or over pergolas, but very good flowering can be obtained from pot-grown specimens which have their shoots trained around wires or canes. Plants should be kept on the dry side in winter and watered well in summer when they require regular high nitrogen feeds. Good cultivars in addition to those mentioned in the chapter on the display glasshouse (see page 81): *B.* 'Miss Manila', with clear orange bracts fading to pink; 'Mahara Off

Abutilon × *milleri*

A frost-free glasshouse, where winter temperatures at night range from 4–10°C (40–50°C) and rise during the day to 13°C (55°F) or more, provides the perfect environment for conservatory plants that originate from cool temperate zones.

White', with double white, pink-tipped bracts; 'Mahara Orange', with double orange bracts fading to pink; 'Mahara Pink', with double pink bracts; and 'Mahara Red', with double red-purple bracts.
Size H: 3–7m/10–23ft. **Season of interest** Summer. **Propagation** Softwood and semi-ripe cuttings in spring and summer.

Cineraria Brilliant
Series

Calamondin see under *Citrus*

Calceolaria

These South American plants are available as annuals and small shrubs in cultivation, and are grown for their unusual, inflated pouch-like flowers which are produced between spring and summer.

C. × *herbeohybrida* (slipper flower) are raised as biennials for their large, bright flowers, available in a wide range of colours. They make good small pot plants suitable for a glasshouse display or bright window sill. C. *integrifolia* (syn. C. *rugosa*) makes a small shrub which is best grown as a half-hardy plant for bedding out in the garden in summer. It requires a sunny position where it will produce clusters of bright yellow flowers in the summer.
Size H: 20–120cm/8in–4ft; S: 15–60cm/6in–2ft. **Season of interest**

Spring to summer. **Propagation** Seed of biennial species; seed, softwood and semi-ripe cuttings of perennials in spring to summer.

Cape cowslip see *Lachenalia*

Cestrum see under
Temperate glasshouse

Chilean bell flower see
Lapageria rosea

Cineraria × hybrida
syn. *Pericallis × hybrida*

These compact flowering pot plants are grown as biennials and produce bright daisy flowers in late winter and spring. Seed selections are available, generally in mixed colours including red, blue, pink and white. Superb Series makes large flowered plants with bicoloured petals. Gaytime Mixture is winter flowering and produces neat plants, making it a good window sill plant.

Special care must be taken when watering *Cineraria* in flower. Plants may wilt in bright sunshine but still be moist at the roots. In such cases, it is best to dampen the foliage.
Size H: 25–45cm/10in–1½ft; S: 15–30cm/6in–1ft. **Season of interest** Winter to spring flowering. **Propagation** Seed from mid-summer through to autumn.

Citron see under *Citrus*

Citrus

Oranges, lemons and limes, grown for their edible fruits and sweet-smelling, white flowers, have been raised successfully in the protection of glasshouses for a few hundred years. They require a minimum temperature of 5–10°C (41–50°F), although plants grown at the lower temperature may drop their leaves in winter and should be kept drier. Growth will resume as conditions improve in spring. Plants are best grown in clay pots or wooden tubs which give them more stability if they are placed outside the glasshouse in summer. Citrus plants are generally easy to raise but tend to suffer from many pests, scale insects and mealy bugs being the worst (see page 57). Plants can be grown from pips but you will have more success if you obtain good named cultivars, often available as grafted plants. Prune in late winter, thinning out crossing branches and shortening half the growths by 75 per cent.

× *Citrofortunella* (calamondin) is a compact evergreen shrub grown for the ornamental value of its small 5cm (2in) fruit and white flowers in winter. The fruit can be used to make marmalade. An attractive variegated form is available with golden leaf markings.

Citrus aurantium (seville orange or bitter orange) produces a tree in the open ground but may be restricted to a shrub in pots. This ornamental plant with its large flowers and coarse orange fruit is used commercially in marmalade production.

Citrus limon (lemon) is a shrub or small tree but well-established plants can be restricted in containers. 'Meyer' is a prolific cultivar with medium-sized, smooth-skinned fruit. 'Variegata' has leaves with grey and gold irregular margins and green and yellow striped fruit.

Citrus medica (citron) makes a large shrub if kept pruned and is grown for its massive fruits which are made into candied peel.

Citrus reticulata (mandarin orange) has medium-sized sweet fruit.

Citrus sinensis (sweet orange) 'Jaffa' has large juicy fruit and is easy to peel.

Size H: 2–5m/6½–16ft; S: 1.5–3m/5–10ft. **Season of interest** All year. **Propagation** Seed in spring; semi-ripe heel cuttings in summer for named cultivars.

Clianthus puniceus
(Lobster claw)

This broad, sprawling shrub from New Zealand has attractive silky, evergreen foliage divided into leaflets and drooping racemes of conspicuous flowers in spring and summer. It grows well in pots trained against wires on the glasshouse wall or as a short standard plant. Prune after flowering to encourage fresh growth. 'Albus' (also sold as 'White Heron') has white flowers; 'Flamingo' pink flowers; 'Red Cardinal' red flowers.
Size H: to 5m/16ft; S: to 2m/6½ft. **Season of interest** Flowers in late

spring and early summer. **Propagation** Semi-ripe cuttings soon after flowering.

Cytisus canariensis
syn. *Genista canariensis*

This graceful broom with its trifoliate leaves on lax stems bears clusters of fragrant, yellow, pea-like flowers in spring and summer. If planted out in the glasshouse border, it will make a large evergreen shrub, but it is also a successful small- and medium-sized pot and container plant. The red spider mite is a major pest of all plants in this family.
Size H and S: to 3m/10ft. **Season of interest** Winter and early spring. **Propagation** Semi-ripe heel cuttings in summer.

Dicksonia antarctica see under Ferns, Temperate glasshouse

Genista canariensis see *Cytisus canariensis*

Jasminum
(Jasmine)

This large genus of shrubs and climbers can be restricted to pots or grown in the glasshouse border, where they will require wires or stakes along which the wiry shoots can be supported or trained. Most of the species have attractive, dark green leaves which show off the delicate, sweetly scented flowers. *J. angulare* has pinnate leaves and clusters of highly

scented white flowers from summer to early winter. *J. grandiflorum* is a twining species grown for its sweetly scented flowers in summer. *J. mesnyi* is a scrambling climber requiring occasional tying-in to keep it in place. It has semi-double, yellow flowers in late winter and spring. *J. polyanthum* is a good climbing jasmine with very fragrant, white flowers, flushed pink when in bud. *J. sambac* is a stocky climber for the temperate glasshouse as it prefers a minimum temperature of 10°C (50°F). Its flowers have a very sweet scent. The double 'Grand Duke of Tuscany' has flowers similar to miniature gardenias.
Size H: 2–3m/6½–10ft. **Season of interest** Mostly spring and summer. Some species produce flowers all year round. **Propagation** Seed in spring; semi-ripe and leaf-bud cuttings in spring and summer.

Citrus limon 'Meyer'

Plumbago auriculata

Lachenalia
(Cape cowslip)

This useful group of small, South African, bulbous plants produces curved, strap-like leaves and long bell flowers on 15cm (6in) long stems.

    L. aloides is the most widely available species, producing pendulous flowers 2.5cm (1in) long in a variety of colours. *L. aloides* var. *aurea* has soft yellow flowers; 'Nelsonii' bright yellow flowers with green tips; and *L. aloides* var. *quadricolor* red and yellow flowers.

Size H and S: to 15cm/6in. **Season of interest** Late winter to spring flowering. **Propagation** Seed in spring; division of bulbs in early autumn; leaf cuttings in late autumn.

Lapageria rosea
(Chilean bell flower)

This climbing plant has thin, wiry stems and waxy, bell-shaped flowers in late summer and autumn. It likes cool conditions and is ideal for a shady conservatory that does not heat up too much in summer, although it will survive on an outside wall in areas with mild winters. A good pot-grown specimen will eventually require a 30cm (12in) container, growing up a wigwam of 1.8m (6ft) canes. Cultivars are available with white, red and pink flowers. Propagation by seed usually produces red flowered forms; cultivars such as the clear pink 'Nash Court' are best propagated by layering shoots.

Size H: to 3m/10ft. **Season of interest** Flowers in late summer to autumn. **Propagation** Seed and layering of shoots in spring.

Lemon see under *Citrus*

Lobster claw see *Clianthus puniceus*

Mandarin orange see under *Citrus*

Mimosa see under *Acacia*

Pellaea rotundifolia see under Ferns, Temperate glasshouse

Pericallis × *hybrida* see *Cineraria* × *hybrida*

Plumbago auriculata
syn. *P. capensis*

This lax shrub produces sky-blue flowers all summer. In temperatures down to 5°C (41°F) it can be regarded as semi-evergreen, producing new vigorous shoots in spring. It is best grown as a climber in pots with the support of a cane or trained to wires up a glasshouse wall. It is also frequently grown as a summer bedding plant when the trained growth produces a column of foliage and flowers. Remove faded flowers in late summer and cut back shoots prior to fresh growth in late winter. *P. auriculata alba* has white flowers with paler leaves than the blue-flowered species.

Size H: 3–6m/10–20ft. **Season of interest** Flowers in summer. **Propagation** Softwood cuttings in spring; semi-ripe cuttings in late summer.

Polystichum falcatum see under Ferns, Temperate glasshouse

Poor man's orchid see *Schizanthus*

Primula

Grown as biennial and perennial plants for their late winter and spring flowers (see page 91 for cultivation), primulas are ideal plants for the cool conservatory, shaded from direct sunlight in spring to prevent sun flag. They grow best in soilless compost and should never be allowed to dry out. Serious pests include glasshouse leafhopper and vine weevil (see page 57 for their control).

    P. 'Kewensis', a hybrid between *P. verticillata* and *P. floribunda*, produces whorls of yellow flowers on stems up to 30cm (1ft) high. *P. malacoides* has

attractive, scalloped, rounded leaves and flower spikes clothed in whorls of dainty flowers. Double and single forms are available in colours ranging from white and pink to lavender and red. *P. obconica* produces large ovate leaves up to 10cm (4in) long covered with fine hairs, which can cause skin rashes. Flowers measure up to 2.5cm (1in) across and are produced on stalks up to 17cm (7in) high in an assortment of colours. *P. × polyantha* is a group of hardy hybrids flowering in early spring that has been freely hybridized with *P. vulgaris*, *P. veris* and *P. juliae* to create a host of vigorous plants with large flowers in a wide range of colours.
Size H and S: 20–30cm/8in–1ft. **Season of interest** Winter and spring flowering. **Propagation** Seed in summer; division in autumn.

Pteris cretica see under Ferns, Temperate glasshouse

Schizanthus
(Poor man's orchid)
This most useful flowering biennial pot plant can flower in winter and spring from seed sown in late summer, or in summer from seed sown in early spring (see page 91 for further cultural details). Both tall and dwarf cultivars are grown for their ferny foliage and beautifully marked flowers, in shades from white to red.
Size H: 30–120cm/1–4ft; S: 30–60cm/1–2ft. **Season of interest** Spring and summer flowering. **Propagation** Seed in spring or late summer.

Seville orange see under *Citrus*

Sprekelia formosissima
(Aztec lily)
The strap-shaped leaves up to 30cm (1ft) long and striking red flowers up to 10cm (4in) long are both produced in spring. Plants should be watered and fed until the autumn when the bulbs should be dried off for winter.
Size H: 15–35cm/6–14in: S: 12–15cm/4¾–6in. **Season of interest** Spring flowering. **Propagation** Seed in spring; division of bulbs in autumn.

Sweet orange see under *Citrus*

Tritonia crocata
This South African bulbous plant has narrow, pale green leaves and small, orange-red, trumpet flowers borne on wiry stems. Corms are potted in autumn with five or six corms per 13cm (5in) pot. It requires a frost-free glasshouse as the foliage is produced in winter before the flowering stems, which appear in spring. Dry off the corms once the foliage starts to die down in early summer.
Size H: to 30cm/1ft; S: to 20cm/8in. **Season of interest** Spring flowering. **Propagation** Seed in spring; division of corms at potting in autumn.

Veltheimia
Also from South Africa, this group of medium-sized bulbous plants has wavy edged, strap-shaped leaves and drooping, tubular flowers borne on

stout stems. Repotting should take place in summer after flowering. The evergreen species V. *bracteata* with pink-purple flowers should not be given a dry rest period but V. *capensis*, with pale pink flowers tipped green, should be given a dry summer rest.
Size H: to 45cm/1½ft; S: to 30cm/1ft. **Season of interest** Spring flowering. **Propagation** Seed in spring; division in summer.

Wattle see *Acacia*   *Primula* 'Kewensis'

Temperate glasshouse

Adiantum raddianum
see under Ferns

Angels' trumpets see *Brugmansia*

Asplenium bulbiferum
see under Ferns

Blechnum gibbum see under Ferns

Button fern see *Pellaea rotundifolia*
under Ferns

Clivia miniata

Brugmansia
syn. *Datura*
(Angels' trumpets)

These vigorous shrubby plants are grown for their exotic trumpet flowers produced in summer. Left to their own devices they will soon outgrow most small glasshouses, but luckily they respond well to pot culture and may be pruned back to 30–60cm (1–2ft) in late winter. Plants can survive cool winter conditions if kept bone dry and should be cut back in late winter and brought into warm conditions to encourage growth. Pot-grown plants can be trained as standards and placed outside the glasshouse for a patio display in the summer. Keep the plants in a sheltered position out of direct sunlight as the large leaves scorch easily in hot, dry conditions. These plants are poisonous to humans but, unfortunately, not to red spider mites which are a persistent problem.

B. × *candida* 'Knightii' is a very good double-flowered white cultivar, with a wonderful evening scent. *B.* 'Grand Marnier' is a vigorous cultivar, producing in the open ground shoots up to 3m (10ft) in one season, which make it so top-heavy that it requires staking. Its size is compensated for by magnificent, peach-coloured trumpets more than 30cm (1ft) long. *B. sanguinea* makes a smaller plant than the other species, easily restricted to a 25cm (10in) pot and, if pruned, will grow no taller than 1.8m (6ft). Flowers are 20cm (8in) long with yellow trumpets turning to orange-scarlet at the trumpet mouth.
Size H and S: 3–11m/10–36ft. **Sea**son of interest Summer to autumn flowering. **Propagation** Seed in spring; softwood and semi-ripe cuttings in early summer.

Cape primrose see *Streptocarpus*

Cestrum

Although these plants will survive cooler conditions, I prefer to grow them in the temperate glasshouse as they will keep their leaves over winter and continue to grow and flower, providing useful winter colour. Most species make large shrubs if planted in the glasshouse border but are easily restricted by pruning and pot cultivation. Pruning can be carried out at any time but I prefer not to do so in winter. Flowers are produced in profusion at the tips of current growth. They can be grown as shrubby climbers by tying shoots to upright posts or horizontal wires.

C. aurantiacum has fresh green foliage and panicles (large, branched, flower clusters) of orange flowers. *C. elegans* has larger leaves than *C. aurantiacum* up to 10cm (4in) long, which are covered with short, felt-like hairs. It produces red-purple, tubular flowers in profusion.
Size H and S: 2–3m/6½–10ft. **Sea**son of interest Flowers mainly in late spring and summer but additional flowers appear in winter. **Propaga**tion Semi-ripe cuttings in summer.

Christmas cactus see
Schlumbergera × *buckleyi*

Clivia

These attractive temperate glasshouse plants grow and flower well in the restrictions of a pot. They have evergreen, strap-shaped leaves, up to 60cm (2ft) long, which are produced in clumps from thick, fleshy roots. Flowers are funnel-shaped, borne in umbels on a stalk above the leaves. Plants are best left undisturbed until the pot is overcrowded with growth when they can be potted on or divided up into separate clumps. Flowering takes place in late spring and is enhanced by a cooler period in the autumn. Clivias are tolerant plants and thrive in shady conditions.

C. miniata has wide, funnel-shaped, orange flowers and leaves up to 6cm (2¼in) wide. 'Aurea' has lemon-yellow flowers and 'Striata' striped yellow, variegated leaves and orange flowers. *C. nobilis* has narrower leaves than *C. miniata* and umbels of tubular, curved flowers which are red with green tips.
Size H: to 60cm/2ft; S: to 90cm/3ft.
Season of interest: Spring or summer flowering. **Propagation** Seed in spring; division after flowering.

Columnea

This group of tropical and temperate woody plants is frequently epiphytic (grows on large trees or shrubs but uses them solely as supports) in its native woodland habitat which is warm and moist. Most species have pendulous stems and their striking, flared, tubular flowers borne along the stems are displayed to best effect in hanging baskets.

C. × banksii has small, glossy, green leaves and scarlet flowers and is the easiest type of *Columnea* to grow. *C. gloriosa* (goldfish plant) has grey-green leaves covered with short hairs, and large fiery-red flowers with a yellow throat.
Size H and S: average 60cm/2ft. **Season of interest** Winter to spring flowering. **Propagation** Softwood cuttings after flowering.

Cyrtanthus purpureus
syn. *Vallota speciosa*
(Scarborough lily)

The long narrow leaves of this bulbous plant measure up to 60cm (2ft) long and persist all year. Scarlet, funnel-shaped flowers are produced on stems above the foliage in late summer and autumn. Repot in spring only if necessary as crowded bulbs tend to flower best.
Size H: 30–60cm/1–2ft; S: 30–45cm/1–1½ft. **Season of interest** Flowers in late summer and autumn. **Propagation** Seed and division of bulbs in spring.

Cyrtomium falcatum see *Polystichum falcatum* under Ferns

Datura see *Brugmansia*

Dicksonia antarctica see under Ferns

Dipladenia see *Mandevilla*

Brugmansia × candida 'Knightii'

A temperate glasshouse, with a winter night temperature range of 10–15°C (50–60°F), rising to over 18°C (65°F) during the day, is ideal for plants from warm temperate and cool subtropical zones.

Ferns

Ferns are mostly shade-loving, woodland plants, requiring moist humid conditions out of direct sunlight, which makes them ideal foliage plants for the shady glasshouse. All the ferns mentioned here have similar cultural requirements although their temperature preferences may differ, and these I have noted. However, all of them will grow successfully in the temperate glasshouse. Ferns come in all sizes, from the small, ground-dwelling button fern to towering tree ferns.

Blechnum gibbum

spicuous black midrib. Leaf bases form a funnel-shaped nest, hence the common name.

Blechnum gibbum is a temperate or tropical growing plant which makes a miniature tree fern, with a narrow trunk up to 90cm (3ft) tall, topped by a rosette of spreading fronds, each up to 60cm (2ft) long.

Dicksonia antarctica is one of the hardiest tree ferns, surviving outside in mild climates, but otherwise is suitable for an unheated or cool glasshouse. Large, well-established specimens may attain a height of up to 5m (16ft), making striking plants with their thick trunks covered with fine, brown roots and their spreading fronds as long as 3m (10ft). Plants can be raised in pots or planted in the glasshouse soil. Their trunks need damping down at least twice a day in the summer.

Nephrolepis cordifolia and *N. exaltata* are the two most common species of *Nephrolepis* grown in the temperate glasshouse. *N. cordifolia* is a tufted plant with rounded tubers and narrow fronds up to 60cm (2ft) long with many parallel toothed leaflets. *N. exaltata* 'Bostoniensis' (boston fern), is also tufted but without tubers. It produces long fronds measuring 60–120cm (2–4ft) with narrow leaflets which look most attractive spilling gracefully over a hanging basket.

Pellaea rotundifolia (button fern) makes a small plant suitable for the cool glasshouse. Fronds measure up to

Propagation can be from fertile, dust-like spores sown on the surface of moist compost, but it will take some time for full-sized plants to develop. Many tufted and rhizomatous ferns can be propagated by division; some species, such as *Asplenium bulbiferum*, produce plantlets on the leaves which can be separated and grown on.

Adiantum raddianum (maidenhair fern) is grown in temperate or tropical conditions for its elegant, leafy fronds with jet-black stems set against pale green, triangular leaflets. 'Fragrantissimum' is a commonly grown cultivar with large leaflets.

Asplenium bulbiferum (mother spleenwort) is a temperate growing fern with large, arching, dissected fronds (90cm/3ft) bearing bulbils, which later develop into plants. *A. nidus* (bird's nest fern) is a tropical growing plant with large (90cm/3ft) glossy, strap-shaped, green leaves with a con-

30cm (1ft) long with rounded to oblong, dark green leaflets.

Phlebodium aureum 'Glaucum', syn. *Polypodium aureum* 'Glaucum', (hare's foot fern) is a tropical epiphytic plant with a creeping rhizome covered with brown scales. It produces long, leathery, mid-green fronds which grow to 60cm (2ft).

Platycerium bifurcatum (stag's horn fern) is a temperate and tropical epiphytic fern with large reflexed, kidney-shaped, sterile fronds and branched, drooping, fertile fronds, bearing brown patches of spores on the underside of the frond tips. Plants should be grown in hanging baskets or tied to a slab of wood or tree fern. They require damping down at least twice a day in summer.

Polystichum falcatum, syn. *Cyrtomium falcatum*, (japanese holly fern) can be grown in a cool or temperate glasshouse. It has coarse, dark green fronds up to 45cm (1½ft) long, with triangular toothed leaflets.

Pteris cretica albolineata (ribbon fern) is suitable for the cool and temperate glasshouse. It has fronds up to 45cm (1½ft) long with three to five terminal leaflets measuring up to 13cm (5in), each with a central white band.

Size H: 10cm–5m/4in–16ft; S: 15cm–6m/6in–20ft. **Season of interest** Many species have attractive foliage all year round. **Propagation** Spores when available; division of rhizomes in late winter.

Hare's foot fern see *Phlebodium aureum* under Ferns

Hedychium gardnerianum
(Kahili ginger)

This rhizomatous plant produces stems with canna-like leaves 45cm (1½ft) long. The sweetly scented, yellow flowers which develop in summer, are borne in spikes at the top of the shoots. Hedychiums can withstand cool glasshouse conditions but must be kept dry and the foliage cut down to the surface rhizome in winter. Raised in temperate conditions the shoots and foliage will continue to grow and watering is required. Plants can be grown in the glasshouse border or in pots, and respond well to a nutritious compost and regular feeds.
Size H: 1.5–2m/5–6½ft; S: from 75cm/2½ft. **Season of interest** Summer to autumn flowering. **Propagation** Seed and division in spring when growth resumes.

Hibiscus

Hibiscus will withstand cool temperate conditions in winter although they will drop their leaves and should be kept on the dry side until the warmer spring temperatures. (In tropical conditions they will grow and flower all year round.) Hibiscus are attractive to pests, and can suffer from scale insects, mealy bugs and aphids (see page 57).

H. rosa-sinensis is grown for its flamboyant flowers, borne on the cur-

rent year's growth. Pot-grown plants will reach up to 2m (6½ft) in 30cm (12in) pots and are easily kept to size by spring pruning. There are many cultivars available with large single, semi-double and double-petalled flowers 10–15cm (4–6in) in diameter. 'Cooperi' is a red-flowered cultivar with variegated grey, white and green foliage. 'Orange Eye' has single, yellow flowers and 'Powder Puff' double, raspberry-red flowers. *H. schizopetalus* is a vigorous species with long arching shoots, best trained as a climber so that the delicate, pink flowers hang below the foliage.
Size H and S: 1.5–3m/5–10ft. **Season of interest** Summer and autumn flowering. **Propagation** Semi-ripe cuttings in summer.

Hoya see under Tropical glasshouse

Hymenocallis × festalis

The parents of this large bulbous plant are native to the Americas. It produces large, strap-shaped leaves up to 60cm (2ft) long and flowers like large, white, spidery daffodils on long stems above the leaves. Flowering takes place in spring and summer, and plants should be watered freely while in growth but kept drier in winter. Pot the bulbs in early spring, with the neck of the bulb just above the surface of the compost.
Size H: to 75cm/2½ft; S: 30–45cm/1–1½ft. **Season of interest** Spring and summer flowering. **Propagation** Seed and division of bulbs in spring.

Ipomoea acuminata
syn. *Pharbitis learii*
(Morning glory)

This perennial climber from tropical America can be grown successfully either in a large pot or in the glasshouse border, trained up canes or a vertical wire. From late spring to autumn it produces a continual show of stunning, bright blue, saucer-shaped flowers which fade to magenta.
Size H: to 5m/16ft. **Season of interest** Late spring to autumn flowering. **Propagation** Seed, semi-ripe stem cuttings and leaf-bud cuttings in spring and summer.

Hibiscus rosa-sinensis 'Mary Wallace'

Passiflora caerulea

Japanese holly fern see *Polystichum falcatum* under Ferns

Kahili ginger see *Hedychium gardenerianum*

Kalanchoe

The tubular flowers of this genus of succulent plants are produced in winter to early spring as a period of short days is needed to initiate flowering. Plants should be grown in full sun and allowed to dry out between waterings.

K. blossfeldiana is a small shrubby plant growing to 30cm (1ft), with glossy, oval leaves and 1cm (½in) long tubular flowers borne in clusters at the shoot tips. There are several cultivars bearing red, orange or yellow flowers. *K. manginii* has small leaves borne on thin wiry stems, bearing a profusion of bright red flowers.

Plants are best grown in hanging baskets so that the stems cascade over the basket. *K. pumila* has pink-grey, powder-coated leaves. Clusters of metallic pink flowers set against the foliage make this a most attractive plant.
Size H: 30–75cm/1–2½ft; S: 15–45cm/6in–1½ft. **Season of interest** Winter to spring flowering. **Propagation** Softwood and semi-ripe cuttings in late spring.

Maidenhair fern see *Adiantum raddianum* under Ferns

Mandevilla
syn. *Dipladenia*

This group of evergreen vigorous climbers produces clusters of showy flowers from the current year's growth. Plants grow well in pots with their shoots trained up a wigwam of bamboo canes. Prune to keep the plants in shape in late winter before new growth resumes. Cut stems produce a white latex which stops after a short period. *M. × amabilis* 'Alice du Pont' is the showiest cultivar with large, vivid pink flowers.
Size H: 3m/10ft. **Season of interest** Summer. **Propagation** Semi-ripe cuttings in early summer.

Morning glory see *Ipomoea acuminata*

Mother spleenwort see *Asplenium bulbiferum* under Ferns

Nephrolepis see under Ferns

Passion flower see *Passiflora*

Passiflora
(Passion flower)

These climbers with their thin, wiry stems and three- and five-lobed leaves climb by means of tendrils which grow from the leaf axils. Passion flowers may be grown in pots up canes, or on horizontal wires stretched between the eaves of the glasshouse. Flowers have a curious structure with reflexed petals and sepals, and a ruff of coloured filaments. The sexual flower parts are extended away from the rest of the flower on a central stalk. Flowering usually takes place from late spring to summer. Many of the species produce edible swollen berries (passion-fruit) which are ready to eat once they start to shrivel.

P. caerulea has attractive blue flowers and is the hardiest species, withstanding periods of frost. The cultivar 'Constance Elliott' has white flowers. *P. antioquiensis* has three-lobed leaves and produces pendulous, rose-red flowers, sometimes followed by edible fruit. *P. × caponii* 'John Innes' is a vigorous climber with coarse, fleshy flowers with pink-red, cupped petals and sepals and long, striped, purple-white filaments, and makes a successful pot plant.
Size H: 3–5m/10–16ft. **Season of interest** Late spring to summer. **Propagation** Leaf-bud cuttings in spring and summer.

Pellaea rotundifolia see under Ferns

Pharbitis learii see
Ipomoea acuminata

Phlebodium aureum see under Ferns

Platycerium bifurcatum
see under Ferns

Polypodium aureum see
Phlebodium aureum under Ferns

Polystichum falcatum
see under Ferns

Pteris cretica see under Ferns

Ribbon fern see *Pteris cretica*
under Ferns

Scarborough lily see *Cyrtanthus
purpureus*

Schlumbergera × *buckleyi*

(Christmas cactus)

This epiphytic, temperate forest cactus has stems made up of flattened pads with toothed margins, and tubular flowers with reflexed petals which are produced in early and mid-winter. The arching stems make this cactus particularly suitable for hanging baskets. 'Gold Charm' has pale yellow-gold flowers; 'Noris' red-purple flowers; and 'Westland' flowers in rosy red shades.
Size H: to 30cm/1ft; S: to 60cm/2ft.
Season of interest Early to mid-winter flowering. **Propagation** Cuttings by removing and rooting succulent pads in spring and summer.

Stag's horn fern see *Platycerium
bifurcatum* under Ferns

Streptocarpus

(Cape primrose)

These clump-forming plants usually have brittle, fleshy, strap-shaped, dark green leaves, which are often covered with fine hairs. However, some species have only one large leaf throughout their lives while others are shrubby with many small, ovate leaves. Plants must be kept moist at the roots and out of direct sunlight and watered with care as cold water will mark the leaves.

S. primulifolius is a clump-forming type with strap-shaped leaves and funnel-shaped, light blue flowers with dark blue stripes on the lower lip. *Streptocarpus* × *hybridus* cultivars include 'Albatross', with pure white flowers; 'Constant Nymph', with purple-blue flowers with a white throat; 'Fiona', with pink flowers; 'Paula', with reddish purple flowers. Popular hybrid seed mixes are Concord, Triumph and Wiesmoor.
Size H: 15–30cm/6in–1ft; S: 30–45cm/1–1½ft. **Season of interest** Spring to summer flowering. **Propagation** Seed in mid-winter; leaf

and softwood cuttings of shrubby species in late winter.

Tibouchina urvilleana

syn. *T. semidecandra*

This long-branched shrub is suitable for training against a wall or, if pinched, grown in pots. Plants have pairs of ovate, pointed and velvety leaves with conspicuous sunken, parallel veins, typical of this plant family. The flowers in spring and summer are a most striking dark, violet-blue, 7cm (2¾in) in diameter.
Size H: 3–5m/10–16ft; S: 90cm–3m/3–10ft. **Season of interest** Spring and summer flowering. **Propagation** Softwood cuttings in spring; semi-ripe heel cuttings in summer.

Vallota speciosa see *Cyrtanthus
purpureus*

Tibouchina urvilleana

Tropical glasshouse

Adiantum raddianum see under Ferns, Temperate glasshouse

___

Allamanda cathartica

(Golden trumpet)

This vigorous, evergreen, scrambling climber, which requires supports to climb, has lanceolate leaves in whorls of four around the stem. If shoots are left to cascade down, the yellow trumpet-shaped flowers are shown off to full effect. Cold draughts may cause plants to drop their flowers. Allamandas are often sold as flowering shoot tips in florists' shops. 'Hendersonii' is a good choice of cultivar with its large, golden yellow flowers in bloom from summer through to autumn. Plants should be pruned back to the main shoots in late winter before fresh spring growth.

Size H: to 5m/16ft. **Season of interest** Flowers from summer to autumn. **Propagation** Semi-ripe cuttings in summer.

Plants from tropical and subtropical regions require a minimum winter temperature at night of 15°C (60°F) which rises during the day to 22°C (72°F) or more. The high humidities which these plants usually enjoy can be maintained by regularly damping down the glasshouse floor on sunny days.

Angels' wings see *Caladium × hortulanum*

___

Blechnum gibbum see under Ferns, Temperate glasshouse

___

Bleeding heart vine see *Clerodendrum thomsoniae*

___

Caladium × hortulanum

(Angels' wings)

These flamboyant tropical foliage plants, some with large 45cm (1½ft) heart-shaped leaves, come in a rainbow of different colours and shades. Plants are dormant in winter when the tubers should be partially dried off and stored above 10°C (50°F). They should then be potted up into a free-draining, rich compost in late spring and forced in a warm place, such as a polythene tent, ideally up to 25°C (77°F). Tubers will start to shoot quickly and pots should be placed on the open glasshouse bench as soon as the first leaves open. If plants are watered and fed freely throughout the growing season, they will produce good, large leaves. Plants will start to die back in mid-autumn. Cultivars include: 'Candidum Junior', with white leaves traced with green; 'Pink Beauty', with marbled pink and green leaves; 'Red Flash', with bright red markings.

Size H: 30–90cm/1–3ft; S: 60–90cm/2–3ft. **Season of interest** Late spring to autumn. **Propagation** Offsets and division of tubers in spring at potting.

Clerodendrum thomsoniae

(Bleeding heart vine)

This evergreen climber is grown for its clusters of white bracts and scarlet flowers which make a vivid display in summer. Plants are easily grown in pots and growths can be trained around a framework of canes.

Size H: 2–4m/6½–13ft. **Season of interest** Spring to summer flowering. **Propagation** Softwood cuttings in spring.

___

Columnea see under Temperate glasshouse

___

Ctenanthe

This medium-sized foliage plant likes shady conditions and a free root-run to reach full size. Plants will grow well in 23cm (9in) pots but stay more compact in smaller containers.

C. lubbersiana is a rhizomatous plant producing oblong leaves with yellow and green mottling. *C. oppenheimiana* 'Tricolor' is a tufted plant which can grow up to 60cm (2ft) in pots. The leaves are lanceolate, 30cm (1ft) long and striped green, cream and grey with a red underside.

Size H: 45–90cm/1½–3ft; S: 60–120cm/2–4ft. **Season of interest** All year round foliage colour. **Propagation** Division in spring.

___

Gardenia jasminoides

This shrub has glossy green leaves and sweetly scented, double white flowers, 8cm (3in) in diameter. Plants

can be kept to a manageable size by growing in pots and pruning hard in spring to promote strong new flowering growth. Water and feed plants freely while in summer growth, but reduce frequency of watering in winter.
Size H and S: 60cm–2m/2–6½ft. **Season of interest** Flowers in summer and autumn. **Propagation** Softwood and semi-ripe cuttings in spring and summer.

Golden trumpet see *Allamanda cathartica*

Hoya

Hoyas are tropical and temperate evergreen climbers and shrubby plants with waxy flowers in pendant umbels.

H. bella (miniature wax plant) is ideal for the tropical glasshouse. It makes a small hanging shrub up to 2m (6½ft) long, and has small, pale green, lanceolate leaves, with clusters of white, scented flowers in summer. Plants grow best in small hanging baskets which should be allowed to become almost dry between waterings. The climber *H. carnosa* (wax plant) is also popular for the tropical glasshouse. The leaves are thick, waxy and ovate, and rounded umbels of white flowers which fade to pink are produced throughout the growing season. 'Variegata' has leaves with an irregular yellow edge, and grows well in pots. Large plants will flower for many years with restricted roots aiding flowering.

Size H: 30cm–6m/1–20ft; S: from 30cm/1ft. **Season of interest** Flowers in summer. **Propagation** Semi-ripe cuttings in summer.

Madagascar jasmine see *Stephanotis floribunda*

Philodendron

This tropical climbing plant has a woody stem bearing thick aerial roots, and often large leaves. Plants thrive in humid conditions out of direct sunlight which can scorch the leaves.

P. 'Burgundy' is a striking cultivar with 30cm (1ft) wine-red, arrow-shaped leaves. *P. scandens* (sweetheart plant) is a slender climber with shiny, heart-shaped leaves. As with many philodendrons, it is best grown up a moist, moss pole so that the aerial roots can establish themselves.
Size H: 90cm–3m/3–10ft. **Season of interest** Foliage interest all year round. **Propagation** Leaf-bud, softwood and semi-ripe cuttings in spring and summer.

Phlebodium aureum see under Ferns, Temperate glasshouse

Platycerium bifurcatum see under Ferns, Temperate glasshouse

Spathiphyllum

This perennial, rhizomatous, clump-forming plant produces attractive, stalked, lanceolate leaves. The typical

Caladium × hortulanum 'Pink Beauty'

arum flowers have a graceful, white, sail-like spathe and central spathix (spike-like flower cluster). Plants grow well in pots or below the staging in the tropical house as they do not require a great deal of light. One of the best cultivars is 'Mauna Loa', a compact plant 45–60cm (1½–2ft) tall with large white spathes.
Size H: 30–90cm/1–3ft; S: to 75cm/2½ft. **Season of interest** Spring to autumn flowering. **Propagation** Rhizome division in spring.

Stephanotis floribunda
(Madagascar jasmine)
This evergreen climber is grown for its clusters of white waxy flowers and almost sickly scent. Plants make good pot specimens if the trailing stems are wound around a wigwam of canes.
Size H: 60cm–5m/2–16ft. **Season of interest** Flowers from spring to autumn. **Propagation** Seed in spring; semi-ripe cuttings in summer.

Index

Acknowledgments

The publisher thanks the following photographers and organizations for their kind permission to reproduce the photographs in this book:

1 Erich Crichton; 2–3 Hugh Palmer; 4–5 Jerry Harpur/Elizabeth Whiting and Associates; 6–7 Annette Schreiner; 8 Edinburgh Photographic Library/D. Morrison; 9 Mary Evans Picture Library; 10 Edinburgh Photographic Library/P. Davenport; 11 Philippe Perdereau; 12–13 Clive Nichols; 14 John Glover; 15 John Glover/Garden Picture Library; 16 Philippe Perdereau; 17 Elizabeth Whiting and Associates; 18 above Gary Rogers; 18 below Jacqui Hurst/Boys Syndication; 19 John Glover/Garden Picture Library; 21 Georges Lévêque; 23 Harry Smith Collection; 25 Clive Nichols; 26–7 Eric Crichton; 28 Neil Holmes; 30 Harry Smith Collection; 31 Jerry Harpur/Elizabeth Whiting and Associates; 32 Neil Holmes; 33 Philippe Perdereau; 35 Clive Nichols; 36–7 Andrew Lawson; 38 John Glover; 39 Tim Sandall; 40 Hugh Palmer; 42 John Glover; 43 Eric Crichton; 45 Andrew Lawson; 46 Clive Nichols; 47 Michèle Lamontagne; 49 John Watkins; 50–1 John Glover; 52 Hugh Palmer; 53 John Glover; 54 Eric Crichton; 55 Clive Nichols; 57 John Glover; 58–9 Michèle Lamontagne; 60 Cynthia Woodyard/Garden Picture Library; 62 Photos Horticultural; 63 Harry Smith Collection; 64–5 Photos Horticultural; 66 John Glover; 67 Elizabeth Whiting and Associates; 68 Clive Nichols; 70 Michèle Lamontagne; 71 Hugh Palmer; 72 John Glover; 73 Michèle Lamontagne; 75 Clive Nichols; 77 Georges Lévêque; 79 Photos Horticultural; 80–1 Hugh Palmer; 84 Harry Smith Collection; 86 Harry Smith Collection; 87 Juliette Wade; 88 Bob Challinor/Garden Picture Library; 89 Hugh Palmer; 90–1 Harry Smith Collection; 92 Harry Smith Collection; 93 Philippe Perdereau; 94 Photos Horticultural; 95 Eric Crichton; 97 Harry Smith Collection; 98 Harry Smith Collection; 100–1 Eric Crichton; 102–3 Harry Smith Collection; 104 Neil Holmes; 105 Michèle Lamontagne; 106 Harry Smith Collection; 107 Brian Carter/Garden Picture Library; 108–9 Andrew Lawson; 112 John Glover; 113 S & O Mathews; 114 Michael Boys/Boys Syndication; 115 John Glover; 116 Andrew Lawson; 118 Harry Smith Collection; 119 John Glover; 120 S & O Mathews; 121 Andrew Lawson.

The publisher also thanks: Vanessa Courtier, Barbara Nash and Janet Smy.